The Guide to Standard Grade English

by

George Sutherland, M.A., D.Ed., B.A., M.Ed.

ISBN 0 7169 3147 8

The Scottish Certificate of Education Examination Papers
and the
Grade Related Criteria from the Arrangements
for the Standard Grade English
are reprinted by special permission of
THE SCOTTISH EXAMINATION BOARD.

ROBERT GIBSON · Publisher
17 Fitzroy Place, Glasgow, G3 7SF.

CONTENTS

INTRODUCTION

This book is meant to help pupils in the third and fourth years of school who are either on, or starting a Standard Grade course in English.

Though this is its main intention, it will also be useful to pupils going on afterwards to take the Higher Grade, especially now that it is revised to fit better with Standard Grade. The way of working is very much the same for both Grades, and that is what this book is about — to give clear information and explanation that will help performance, to help you to make the best of your abilities and what you learn from your teachers. For that reason, the book may be of some help to teachers as well, though it is intended for pupils.

Standard Grade courses and examinations together are the most far-reaching revision of education at 14 – 16 for a generation, and are still fairly new to everyone. This book will help **pupils** in particular to find their way through the course and examination system in English, and to come out as survivors. It is the first one to do so.

It does not hope to replace your teachers, or indeed to offer anything in conflict with what is taught in schools. It does set out to give advice, to build your confidence and self-awareness. It offers you essential and authoritative information and advice on the Standard Grade course and examination system.

It is not a 'course book' with practice exercises and past papers (these can be obtained from Robert Gibson & Sons Ltd., Glasgow) for you to attempt. It gives clear, essential information about how the course and the exams work. It will help you to understand your part in the course. It will help you to work better with your teacher, who is your best guide.

Since 1984 it has been possible for all S3 and S4 pupils to take a course in English leading to the Scottish Certificate of Education at Standard Grade. The course will be be new to you, but it will be quite new to your teachers as well. That is why this book is being written — to offer you as much help as is possible in a book, and at the same time to help your teachers by helping you.

The book sets out to explain to you what Standard Grade is all about, what makes it different from the kind of examination that your teachers and your parents have been used to, what you are expected to be able to do at the end of the course, what the examiners expect and what they are looking for. It will also make clear what your certificate will tell others about your abilities and how suited you might be for whatever you choose to do after you leave school.

First of all, then, a little of the background to Standard Grade that will help you to understand why all third and fourth year pupils are going to be involved in it and why it will be useful to know the kind of thinking that has gone into setting it up in place of 'O' Grade.

The important ideas of Standard Grade are:

(i) all pupils should study a balanced curriculum;

(ii) all pupils should sit examinations and gain certificates to show what they can do.

Naturally, there's much more to it than that, but this is meant to be just a 'little bit of background' and we all know that hardly anyone reads the part of any book that is headed 'Introduction'. In fact, it would not be very surprising if you were reading this much later on than when you first picked up this book. This is why later in the book you will find (have found?) several reminders to go back and look at the Introduction.

Out of these two main ideas come two very important things:

    (i) the need for courses to be constructed in the schools by the teachers following guidelines in a book called *Arrangements in English at Standard Grade*, and

    (ii) the need for examinations that were suitable for all pupils.

That is probably enough of the history of Standard Grade, because you are probably much more interested in finding out what you have to do because of it.

CHAPTER 1

STANDARD GRADE — GENERAL INFORMATION

In the parts of this book that deal with the Course, you will find out that because of the two main features of Standard Grade, you will be given the chance to show what **you** can do when **you** choose, rather than show what you **can't** do when the **examiner** chooses.

In the part of the book that deals with the examinations, you will find that the same opportunity is there for you to show what you **can** do when you are making the choices: you will not always be trying to do what the examiner demands, thus tending to uncover what you **can't** do. It's up to you to put on your best performance and offer that to the examiner. For quite a lot of the examination the examiner happens to be your class-teacher, anyway.

Near the beginning of the next chapter you will find a diagram that sets out how, firstly, the coursework you do in class and secondly, the examinations you will sit at the end of fourth year are combined to produce a set of grades for all your work so that this can be reported on your certificate and decide what final grade you will get for English. This will be reported on your certificate as the 'Final Award'. Although the diagram has really got more to do with the examinations and the assessment (grades) for your work, it is in there at the beginning of the course section because it shows how the whole system of Standard Grade fits together to form one complete package covering the two school years you will be doing the course. It shows that the two things, the Course and the Examinations are closely linked together, and this is **very** important to realise if you are to do well at Standard Grade. It is not possible to sit back and do very little during the course and hope you will do well in the examinations at the end: it is also impossible to gain a certificate for your two years' work by simply doing the coursework and not bothering about the exam. The two go together.

You will begin to see that Standard Grade involves you personally in a lot more work and more responsibility for your own work than was ever the case for other examinations. The chapter on the Folio (Chapter 4) will make this very clear to you.

We had better turn to the outline description of what you will have to do for Standard Grade, because all this talk of courses, examinations, folios, grades and the rest of it could become quite puzzling unless we have a better picture of the whole thing. The picture (in words) follows now.

CHAPTER 2

A GENERAL DESCRIPTION

Either just after the S.C.E. exams in May or when you come back to school after the summer holidays at the end of second year, you will find that you have begun a course in English that will last two years, and that at the end of it you will sit examinations and be awarded a certificate. What is printed on it will depend on what subjects you have taken, of course, and on how well you have done. What is important, however, is that you will gain a certificate that will show what you have achieved.

Under *English* there will be grades for Reading, Writing, Talking and also a Final Award for English. The final award is arrived at by combining the 'profile' grades for the 'elements' as they are called. What isn't obvious is how they are combined. Since there are more ways of killing a cat than choking it with cream, it isn't safe to assume that the 'elements' are all equal in weight when 'aggregated' (added up). This is why the diagram is printed below. It is doubly useful because it shows not only the weighting of the 'elements' and how they combine to make the final award, but it gives an outline in diagram form of the course activities.

In 1987, the Standard Grade arrangements were changed so as to make the assessment more straightforward for your teachers. One of the ways in which the examination was made simpler was removing the separate exam in Listening. Although there are not any separate exams in Listening now, there is still a great deal of listening in the course you will follow in your school, and to some extent it will contribute to the overall award you get, because it has quite a strong place still in the discussion part of Talking — and that is worth one-third of the whole value of the exam system

REVISED: 1988 onwards

Diagram A — Elements

Diagram B — How they are assessed

8

Diagram A simply shows the 'elements' ... what you do in the course that is assessed.

Diagram B breaks these down into more detail and shows how they are assessed. This is in one of three ways: 'externally' means by a written examination set by the Examination Board; 'internally' means that it is done by your class-teacher during the course; 'coursework externally' is almost a mixture of these two ways. You do the work in class during the course and then send it in to the Examination Board and it is assessed there.

You can see that in the course you will be reading and writing, as you would expect. You will also be talking (and listening) and this 'element' — Talking — makes up one third of the total value of the grades for the course. What is obvious from the diagram is that quite a lot of the value of the grades comes directly from what you do in the classroom: all of the Talking, for example, comes from the grade awarded you by the school for what you have done over the two years of the course. Half of the value of Reading and half of the value of Writing comes from the grades awarded (this time by the Examination Board) for work done in the class but which is sent in by your school to be graded at the Board. The package that is sent in contains samples of your work in Reading and Writing. This is your **Folio**, and it is largely your responsibility to make sure that it contains the best you have done, and that the contents match what the examiners have asked for. Your teacher will help you with this, of course, but it is a good idea for you to know as much as you can about what is required. You can find out all about that in the new version of the book mentioned already, on page 5, *Revised Arrangements in English*. Your English teacher will have a copy. Some pages from it are reprinted later in this book, because they make clear exactly what you are expected to do in examinations, or explain how your work is assessed. There is also a whole section later in this book on the **Folio** (Chapter 4).

You will have gathered by now that during the course, much of what you do will be assessed by your teachers. This does not mean that you will be sitting endless tests. There is a difference between what is called continuous assessment and what could be called continual assessment.

IT RAINED CONTINUOUSLY.

IT RAINED CONTINUALLY.

Continuous indicates an unbroken sequence. "It rained continuously for three days" means it never stopped raining.

Continual refers to things that happen repeatedly but not constantly.

"It rained continually for three days" means that there were some interruptions.

A dictionary example will not tell you who got wetter: but it will tell you how the assessing of your work will be done. It will be being done all the time. Though the assessment will cover all your work during the two years of the course it does not mean that every scrap of paper with writing on it, or every word you utter will be graded. Teachers will carry out what is called formative assessment. This is a lot less painful than it sounds.

". . . a lot less painful than it sounds."

Basically, it means that when they 'mark' your work, they will be using the chance to teach you how it can be improved as well. You will get used to one of the main ways of working at Standard Grade — the improving or 're-drafting' of your work. This is not simply re-writing a neat copy of what you have done. There is an example of re-drafting later in the book (pages 27 – 28) which shows what can be done to improve almost anything. The sentences you are reading have been re-drafted. I think they are better than the original version, but you can judge for yourself whether the re-drafting has worked. If it has, the few sentences above this will be clear and understandable. The illustration on pages 27 – 28 shows what the paragraph above looked like when I first wrote it.

There is much more information on re-drafting at pages 25 – 29 and warnings in the Folio chapter pages 45 – 48.

CHAPTER 3

THE COURSE — BASIC/ESSENTIAL INFORMATION

The diagram on page 8 does not make clear everything, of course. We need a few more words for that. (Well actually, more than just a few.) These are some of the main features of the Standard Grade course:

1. It lasts two years.
2. It covers four 'modes' of language.
3. It is specially designed for you.
4. It is the same course for all pupils.
5. It is composed of 'units'.
6. It includes continuous and internal assessment.
7. It involves group/class/individual teaching.
8. It calls for re-drafting and storage of your work.
9. It includes your classwork in the assessment.
10. It is completed by external examinations.
11. It leads to a certificate.

You need to know more about each of these features or important characteristics of Standard Grade English, so each one is now explained separately in detail: it's quite long, but if you persist with it, you'll understand better about the Folio and Examination chapters that follow it.

1. Course Length

The course begins at the beginning of your third year and ends at the examinations taken at the end of fourth year. All the work that you do in class during that time and the examinations will count in one way or another towards the final award you gain.

2. The Four Modes of Language

As has already been mentioned, the course will deal with the four 'modes' or kinds of language: reading, writing, talking and listening. Two of these, writing and talking, are 'expressive modes', that is, they are the forms of language that allow you to express yourself, or tell (in speech or writing) other people what you want to communicate to them. The other two, reading and listening, are the 'receptive' modes of language. They allow you to **receive** the communications from others. You could think of it as a two-way radio system, and this would perhaps help you to understand why both the expressive and the receptive modes of language are important: it wouldn't be a very effective two-way or CB system if you were able only to speak, or only to listen. Most communication systems need both sending and receiving to be of any use to us. Think of phones, telex, fax machines, etc.

The little problem we have with the receptive modes, reading and listening, as far as teaching and examining and learning go, is that the only way to find out if they have been working properly is to test them through the expressive modes. I don't know whether you have been listening unless you are able to write down or tell me what you have listened to. There were lots of jokes about how the listening tests would be carried out by the Examination Board, including having the electrodes on the brain and the listening recorded on the spectroscope.

A system not adopted by the Board . . .

The same goes for reading, of course.

Language does not work in the separate compartments that we may imagine when we have to talk of its separate modes. The course will not deal with them separately either. You don't need to be told that when you are working in class you will perhaps read something, a story or a poem or a set of instructions, and if you are to go on to write something connected with it, you will very probably talk about it in groups or pairs or as a class or with your teacher alone, and all of this will have involved listening.

Each of these modes of language will be dealt with later in this book, both in the **Course** sections and again separately in the **Examinations** section. There is now no separate examination in Listening. You can see this by looking back at the two diagrams on page 8.

3. Course Design

The book *Revised Arrangements in English* published by the Scottish Examination Board (SEB), has been mentioned several times already, you will have noticed. This is not surprising, really. It would be very difficult to say anything about the course in Standard Grade English **without** mentioning it. You see, why it is so important is that it explains Standard Grade English courses to all teachers of English. The later parts of it have to do with the regulations for the examinations and do not concern us here, but the earlier part sets out to give advice and information to teachers all over the country about the design of courses. The reason for this is that the basic idea of Standard Grade is that the courses should take account of what pupils need — and that means that the course you are following has been designed and made by the English teachers in your school to fit the needs of pupils in your school. Even though since the revision some materials are provided for the school, it is not all made up somewhere centrally and sent to your school in Bettyhill or Eyemouth or Glasgow or wherever. It should obviously be suitable for you and your classmates, therefore. It might have local material built in to it: whatever it contains, you can be assured that it was made by teachers who know your needs probably better than anyone else does, including yourself.

4. The Unitary Course

In all subjects at Standard Grade, including English, the **examinations** and the awards on the **certificate** are offered at different levels. Most subjects have three levels: Foundation, General and Credit. This applies to English, too.

However, though some subjects offer **courses** which are also very different at each level, this is not the case in English. Notice that I am making a very clear distinction between **examinations** (assessment) and **courses**.

In the school, the course, designed by your teachers, will be what is called **unitary**. That means that it does not have totally different activities and learning, or different content at different levels, but that all pupils do the same kind of things in the course. What you take out of it, and again, what work you produce, will of course be different from what others in the same year-group or even the same class may learn or produce from the same course. Everyone does not have the same ability: everyone has the same opportunity, though. So, although everyone does the same course, it is possible for you and your classmates to gain different levels of award at the end of the course.

Later in this book, when we come to describe the examination system (Chapter 5) you will see that even quite a lot of the examination is the same for all pupils and that the award you gain on your certificate depends on your performance, not only on sitting different levels of examination papers. In fact, quite a lot of your award is based not on examination papers at all but on the work that you do in the classroom and even elsewhere for some of it.

This system is possible in English because the subject is not what we call linear — meaning that what you learn one day does not depend to the same extent on what you learned the day before or the week before, as it tends to do in some other subjects where there is a great deal of dependence on knowledge of the **content** or facts. English isn't entirely concerned with facts. The method of teaching and learning that is used in English depends more on the improvement and extension of the **quality** of what you have learned. Examples are not easy in this area, but let's try to provide one that will help you to understand this rather difficult idea. The example will probably be quite crude, and your teachers of Geography probably won't like it and will think it unfair. Take for example one of the things that you might learn in the Geography department:

The northernmost point of the mainland of Scotland is at Dunnet Head (not John o'Groats).

Quite obviously, that is a fact, and no amount of discussion or argument or opinion is going to alter the truth of that fact, and therefore in a sense there is not a lot more to be said about it. The truth of it can be tested by measurement and direct observation, and it is not possible to come up with a different answer to the question, "Which is the most northerly point of the mainland of Scotland?" You can produce a different answer only if you change the question. Like "What is the most northerly **inhabited** point of the mainland of Scotland?"

Remembering that this is a **very crude** comparison between the way in which learning in English operates and the way in which it operates in some other subjects (not only Geography), let's take something that you might deal with in your English course. For example:

In one of his poems, the Irish poet, Seamus Heaney uses the title *Mid-Term Break*.

Someone could say that this refers to the fact that in the poem a boy is sent for from his school and goes home. He has a break at mid-term. It would be unwise to state as a fact that the poem is called *Mid-Term Break* **because** the boy has a break from school at mid-term. It cannot be a **fact** in the same way as the statement about Dunnet Head. There are other possible reasons for this title for the poem, and the interesting thing about these reasons is that it is perfectly acceptable in English for the reasons to be based on opinion — not only on your teacher's opinion, or on the poet's opinion even: the opinion of the reader (and that includes you and me and all the other people in your class) can be completely valid, provided it can be supported by some evidence from what you have read in the poem, or from something you have heard or read in a completely different situation. In this case, the boy went home at mid-term certainly, but the reason for going home was to attend the funeral of his four-year-old brother, who had been killed in an accident (probably). The little boy's life had been broken in mid-term, or before its natural end. His term of life was not completed; it was broken off short.

It would be possible to go on at length discussing the quality of language and so on, but this was meant to be an example of the way in which English tends to be different from many other subjects in that it is unitary (one course for all pupils). In one case the information is clear and fixed and once you have learned it, you may go on to learn other things that depend upon it; in the other case, the learning is not closed. What you have learned is not very different from what you already knew. What tends to be happening is that the quality of your understanding is being strengthened by repeatedly returning to instances of very similar use of language. What changes is not just the quantity but the quality of your knowledge and understanding. Not only how many things you know, but how well you know many things. This leads to courses in English being designed for pupils of all abilities, doing the same kind of things.

Because the teaching and learning of English works in this way, it tends to allow certain ways of organizing it. In your school, the classes may be organized in a mixed-ability system, or grouped in ways that allow some classes to work in ways that suit the needs of the pupils in them. Some arrangements may have the purpose of aiming more at the Credit and General levels of the examinations than at the General and Foundation levels. There may be other combinations; that is entirely up to the school to decide.

No matter in what way the classes are organized in third and fourth year, all the pupils will be following a **course** that is basically the same for all of them. It is quite important for you to know this. Whatever class group you are in you still have the opportunity to do your best classwork in the course, and then later, because of your performance in the examinations at the end of fourth year (and also during the whole two years of the course), to gain an award **at any level**. You will see how this works when you read a later section of this book on "The Examinations — Presentation" (Chapter 5). It is particularly important to read the section on Reading, where the arrangements are just slightly different.

5. The Units of the Course

It is easy to tell you that the course is made up of "units", but that doesn't help much, does it? They could be kitchen units, Special Units (as at Barlinnie Prison), units of electricity, army units, seating units or whatever.

"Unit" is one of those weasel words when it comes to fixing its meaning. It's like asking,

"How long is a piece of string?"

to which the answer is

"Double half its length", of course.

We still don't know what we wanted to know even though we've had an answer that is just as sensible as the question.

In the *Arrangements in English at Standard Grade* (the book already mentioned on page 5) there is a definition or description of what a unit is: it took a lot of effort to write that description — and when it was written a great many teachers learning about Standard Grade English were glad to see it, because they hadn't been too sure about what it meant up till that time either. Though the business of units in the course is mostly a matter for your teachers, it is necessary for you to know how the course is constructed and how it works and most of all why it is constructed in this way.

How it works is like this: you learn about the language by using it — in reading, writing, speaking and listening, and the unit is a way of grouping activities (things for you to do) in language to allow you to use language naturally, to do real things as opposed to artificial exercises. The units form a kind of framework or "context" as it's called, which brings together various things for you and the class and your teacher to do that all involve using language in situations where it really works. This makes sure that you develop not only your language skills, but also your own self and personality. It also allows your teacher to deal naturally and sensibly with what you do and to learn from the activities contained in the unit, because he or she is involved, too.

So a unit is a way of organising the study and use of language into manageable sets. A single unit may, for example, be based on a novel or story, out of which will grow a variety of things to be done which make you use the language skills of the different "modes". It might require reading the novel or story and other writings connected with it in some way, or discussing incidents or characters or ideas in the story, discussing with a partner or in a group some problem from the story, writing a story of your own which is inspired by the original or connected with it, listening to others in discussion of it, perhaps watching a film or video dramatisation of the story. A unit like that might last for several weeks. During that time you will be using language in many different ways. The important thing though is that you will be **learning by doing**; you will notice that fewer of your lessons in English will consist of your whole class being talked to by your teacher.

By no means all units will be like that. Some may be quite short, perhaps covering only a few English periods and dealing with something quite specific — for example, the particular skills required in writing a summary, or how to construct a questionnaire, or how to use certain kinds of reference books in the school or public library, or even, it was suggested, how to use the comma. One on how **not** to use the comma would be valuable, also.

Whatever the unit is based upon, it will be designed to suit your needs; it will involve you in a variety of language activities; it will bring you into experiences, real and imagined, and ideas that are intended to develop your learning and thinking; it will allow your teacher to help, inform and improve your work in English and it will leave you with something to show for your efforts. Not least, it will be enjoyable and meaningful.

Most units will contain written or printed materials: many will have drawings, photographs, maps, diagrams, extracts and short texts (maybe poems and short stories, etc.) as well as information about what you are to do and for what purpose. There will almost always be choices for you to make within the unit. There will also, of course, be assignments of work of various kinds. You may be asked to read other stories or articles, or carry out research into some subject arising from the unit's materials, or discuss with your group, interview people, write all sorts of things, e.g., letters, new endings, opinions, personal experiences, newspaper or magazine articles. Again, you may have to listen to radio, or record audio tapes or watch video-tapes, visit places or find out things from elsewhere. The possibilities are as wide as your teacher's imagination and limited only by what is possible in your particular school.

What you might not find are artificial situations. Teachers know the story of the two primary schoolgirls out on a 'nature ramble'.

Susan suddenly said,

"Look, Marlyn, there's a wee frog!"

Marlyn took one look at it and said,

"For goodness sake, look away. Don't let on you've seen it or we'll have to write an essay about it."

I have mentioned several times so far that these units will have been designed and made up by your teachers in the English Department. Some of the units you will meet in the course will not be like that, however. Some will have been provided to the school so that if the English Department finds that one or more of these units fits into the course they have arranged for you, they will adopt them and fit them in. You shouldn't be able to see the join.

". . . shouldn't be able to see the join . . ."

I expect that you are beginning to see that a course is made up of units of different kinds, with different purposes and of different lengths. Obviously the units are fitted together into the two-year course so that there is "progression in the learning outcomes". That is jargon language for the simple idea that you learn from each unit and that they demand more as the course continues; they don't just do the same thing over and over again. They are intended to "stretch" you. Not literally, of course. While you probably are stretching during third and fourth year because you are growing, the course is meant to provide for the growth of your mental powers, or if you like, stretch your mind.

In any unit that you tackle in school, you should always know what its purpose is, what you are expected to learn during and from it, and how your work is progressing at the end of it. You should also know how it helped you, what you liked and disliked about it, what you thought could be improved or made clearer to make it better. Your teacher would like to know these things too, and most units will contain some way of letting you report what you thought of it. So that your school's units can be improved or used with other classes you should tell your teacher your views. Politely . . . !

We know that sometimes this is hard to do: not everyone seems to welcome criticism, especially if it is not favourable comment. One of the central ideas of Standard Grade is to help you to be **articulate**, and that means being able and willing to talk to anyone about anything at any time — if you have something worthwhile to say. In the same way that you must know where you are, where you are going in the course and in each unit, you must also know where you have been and what you have done and why. You are to be responsible, too, for your learning and that means that you have to be in shared control of it. In the same way, your teacher requires control of teaching, for which he or she is responsible. The more you know about how the course works, the more confident you will be and the better your work is likely to be.

6. Continuous Assessment

As I hope you've already gathered (see page 10) continuous assessment does not mean that you will be sitting tests each and every day of your life in third and fourth year. School sometimes feels like that, doesn't it?

I remember when I was eleven (about a hundred years ago) and was going up from the Primary School to the Secondary School, I was telling a friend of mine, who was fourteen, that my father was going to buy me a bike for doing well in the exams. My friend said, "If I had got a bike for every exam I've sat I would have a whole shopful of them by now." I didn't believe her then: now I think that she may well have been right.

The Standard Grade course in English needn't be full of examinations or tests at all. It may be that in your school there are exams at the end of each term, or each year, but most of the assessing (i.e. the valuing or measuring of your work) will be what is called **formative** assessment. This is not sore or uncomfortable for you as I've said. Indeed, quite the opposite. It is just the name for what your teacher does as a matter of routine: it is part of the teaching. If you look up "formative" in the dictionary you will find that it says something like

"(Adj.) serving to fashion or form". The verb it comes from is obviously 'to form', and the same dictionary will give, among other meanings of this word, "mould by discipline, train, instruct (person or faculty) ... embody or organize ... frame, make, produce ... etc." The meaning we are interested in is "train, instruct".

We will certainly leave aside the "mould by discipline" meaning, for we all know what **that** kind of discipline used to mean in schools.

It had to do with leather goods usually made in Lochgelly.

In plain language, your teacher uses the opportunity when assessing or 'marking' your work in the class to show you how it can be improved, at the same time noting what you have achieved. It is meant to teach you at the same time as recording your progress so far.

As you can see, this does not need an examination: any of your work, whether in writing or speaking or reading or listening can be assessed in this way painlessly, usually, for you. Working with you directly on your work is a most effective way of teaching and learning: your teacher is **showing** you how to do it, not just telling you. You are **learning by doing**. As I've already said, this is an important feature of Standard Grade English.

Let's hope that your Standard Grade course is not going to be like the famous satirical poem by Alexander Scott about education in Scotland. It is very short, very clear, and very effective:

SCOTCH EDUCATION

Ah tellt ye!

Ah tellt ye!

During the course, most of what you produce or do — your performance — will be informally assessed in this way and will contribute to another kind of assessment which is made sometimes only towards the end of the course, but quite often made also at various points within the course. At the end of a particular unit, for example, would be a likely time for it. This is the kind of assessment that sums up your performance overall, and deals with a large body of work, not just with separate pieces of it. Because it sums up, it is called "Summative Assessment".

This kind of assessment is rather important, because it provides the information for the grades your teacher awards for the internally (i.e. carried out within the school) assessed parts of the course. The whole of the Talking element is assessed internally. Summative assessment also provides your teacher with the information for estimates of the grades he or she thinks you will get in the external examinations. The Examination Board needs these estimates of your performance in Reading and Writing. The reasons for this are explained later in the book at the section dealing with how to survive the examinations (Chapter 5). Estimates are a kind of life-jacket for you.

7. Learning Groups

One of the interesting things you find out if you visit a great many schools over the length and breadth of the country, as I used to do, is that both teachers and pupils tend to think that one school is much the same as any other and that it is therefore "normal". The fact is that schools are different from each other in a surprising number of ways and that it would be very difficult to work out which ones are "normal" and which ones are not. One of the ways in which schools differ from each other is in the way they arrange pupils into classes.

For this reason it is not possible to speak about your school and the way it organizes its teaching groups or classes. It is entirely up to the school to decide which way is best for its pupils and its teachers. Standard Grade courses, however, do depend on certain kinds of arrangements within each class or teaching section.

You could probably agree that schools set up very artificial learning situations. What I mean by that is that in ordinary life outside school, if someone wants to teach or show someone else how to do something, they don't usually gather together 29 other people of exactly the same age, wait for a bell to ring before starting, speak to all the people in the same way regardless of any differences among them and then stop at the sound of a bell exactly 30 or 40 or 45 minutes later.

Of course not ... but this is a travesty, a deliberate and wildly generalized exaggeration of what a school is like, but I'm sure that you get the point: what schools do by way of organizing learning situations is not quite like other learning situations in the world beyond school. Think of how you learned to ride a bike, for example, or how to do your make-up (only if you're a girl?) or to catch fish or to tie your laces. Was it really like learning Maths ? or, for that matter, English?

If there were no such things as schools, they would have to be invented. It really isn't possible for our kind of society to teach people what they have to know by the same methods as we use to learn some of the skills of life like the ones mentioned above. Our society is too specialized for that to be a workable method. Whether it is like that because the school system has made it like that or whether it is the other way round — that schools simply reflect the society in which they are found, is another debate that has gone on for a long time. You see in the papers and on radio and television almost every day that someone is calling for something or other to be taught in the schools. Usually it is something that has caught the attention of the public, or it may be that it is because someone believes that this country will fall behind others unless we train more people to be able to do this, that or the other. The other side of the picture is shown by a famous educationist when he described what he called "The Sabre-Tooth Curriculum". It was about the problems of a fictitious society where pupils were being taught valuable life-skills such as how to trap sabre-toothed tigers. Unfortunately at the time they were being taught these skills, the sabre-toothed tiger had been extinct for quite a long time!

Nevertheless, to return to the point, some of the methods used outwith schools can certainly be used in schools, and in Standard Grade English this is recognized. So, you will find that for some of the time in English you will not be one of a group of 30 or so classmates listening to your teacher teaching you all the same thing at the same time and in the same way. Sometimes you will be one of a small group discussing some topic or problem: you might be working with a partner writing up information you gathered while working together on some kind of investigation. Sometimes you might not even be in the classroom — because you have had to interview someone in another part of the school; the Janitor who is an expert on bee-keeping; or the Head Teacher because he spent his early days in North Africa; or a teacher who was Miss Scotland in 1950, for example.

On the other hand, you alone may be being shown some particular detail of writing by your class-teacher. If you are in a school that has an arrangement for co-operative teaching, you might find yourself in a smaller group with one teacher while the rest of your class is working with another teacher on different work or in the library, involved in research for information needed for the unit they are working on. If this sounds unfamiliar to you, don't be too surprised. By no means all schools have co-operative teaching, or a Learning Support Teacher, or a library, but some do.

Of course, much of this isn't new to you, or even special to Standard Grade or English. You have probably worked in groups or pairs before, especially in the Primary School. Like most pupils of your age, you will have "done the Projects" in the Primary School: you must remember the Dinosaurs, usually followed by the Romans and/or the Vikings! What may be different since you started in the Secondary School is that you may not have worked in groups or pairs in many subjects other than English, and in Standard Grade that situation is likely to continue. You will work this way in English but you may or may not in some of the other subjects you are taking at Standard Grade; more so if you are taking some subjects at Standard Grade and some at Ordinary Grade. This is quite likely to be the case. Standard Grade is being introduced gradually, subject by subject, and English is in the first phase or group of subjects. The others in the first phase are Mathematics, Science and Social and Vocational Studies. After 1991 there won't be any 'O' Grade English.

8. Re-drafting and Storing Your Work

We're still working through the list of the main features of your Standard Grade Course which are listed on page 12 and for which you need basic information at this stage before we go on to look at some of them in detail in the later part of the book. There's not long to go now for there were only 11 features on the list and this is number 8.

One big improvement of the Standard Grade Course in English over, say, Ordinary Grade, is that you are not given a grade for Writing as a result **only** of what you write on one single (usually sunny and beautiful) day in May when you find yourself trapped in an examination hall and are invited to be creative at 9.15 in the morning. As a matter of fact, you will be doing something **quite** like that, but different (see Chapter 5 on *The Examinations*). That, however, will count for only half of your grade for writing: the exam that you do in Reading at about the same time will count for only half of your final grade for Reading. The other two halves ($\frac{1}{2}$ for Writing; $\frac{1}{2}$ for Reading) will come from what you do during the course, and directly from what you send in to the Examination Board to be marked and graded. This work will be a sample chosen by you and by your teacher and will make up your **Folio**. It's a folder of work of different kinds required by the Board so that they can grade your performance in this way. There is a whole chapter later in the book (Chapter 4: *The Folio of Coursework*) dealing with the Folio in detail. It is very important that you understand exactly what is required and that you and your teacher make sure that your Folio meets the exact requirements; the specification. This is explained carefully in the chapter I have just referred to.

The important thing about the work in the Folio as well as all your other written work in the course, is that it can be "re-drafted". Put simply, that means that you will be given the chance, indeed you will be expected to improve your work step by step until you consider it finished and polished, and what you 'hand in' to be assessed is your best, your finished work, the version that you are happy with. There is no limit to the amount of changes and improvements you are allowed to make to the first version of your writing.

Though this might begin to sound to you like a very easy way to do an exam, there are careful rules about it and you must obey them. Otherwise the consequences for you could be disastrous. Re-drafting your work does not mean that your teacher does it for you. Obviously that cannot be; if it was done like that, and you sent it in your Folio for grading, you would not be being given the proper credit for the work; part of the credit would be your teacher's, and that would hardly be fair to you or to other pupils or to those people who 'use' your certificate, (employers, colleges, universities, for example) would it? From the wider point of view, things like that would discredit the whole examination and in the end the public would devalue the Standard Grade Certificate. It really wouldn't be worth having if it could be gained in that way. Apart from anything else, it would be fraud.

No, your teacher, of course, has to take quite a lot of credit for what you have learned by the end of the course: that is what teaching does for you.

The whole purpose of teaching is to help you to be able to do things after the teaching that you couldn't do before you were taught. That's fairly obvious. But the certificate tells others what **you** have been able to do, and how well.

That little digression in certification is not to mislead you into believing that re-drafting is done only for assessment. It is one of the main ways in which you learn to write better. It is an important feature of all the work you do in class and its main purpose is to teach you about writing. Your teacher will use it in the formative assessment that was explained earlier.

The sections on **The Course** and especially **The Folio** will tell you more about re-drafting, naturally, but there are two main ideas to understand at this point in the information process: one is that re-drafting does NOT mean simply making a neat copy of your work in your best writing so that it will look better for the Examination Board marker who has to read it: the other idea you should get clear is that though some pieces of your written work may be just perfect at the first attempt, this is likely to be an unusual event. Each piece of writing can almost certainly be improved by re-drafting. The illustration here shows the kind of thing I mean. The scope for improvement of the first (typed and handwritten) version is clear. The final version is actually on page 11 of this book, so you can now compare the two versions.

Basically, it means that when they 'mark' your work, they will be using the chance to teach you how it can be improved as well. You will get used to one of the main ways of working at Standard Grade -- the improving or 're-drafting' of your work. This is not simply re-writing a neat copy of what you have done.

Cartoon of 'Formative Assessment Chamber'
"a lot less painful than it sounds"

~~There is a section of this book about writing~~ bd example ~~that deals with~~ of ~~redrafting~~ later in the book which ~~and shows you~~ ~~what can be done to improve almost anything~~ ~~you produce.~~ The sentences you are reading have been re-drafted I think t ~~T~~hey are better than the original version, but you can judge ~~later~~ for yourself ~~how good they are!~~ whether the re-drafting has worked. If it has, the few sentences above this will be clear and understandable.

There is an example of re-drafting later in ~~this~~ the book, which shows what can be done to (P. ±0) improve almost anything

In the real world, (I mean the world of work, outside of school, and that doesn't mean that school isn't real: it's only a way of speaking, what people say when they want to make clear that they are talking in really practical terms) people who write for publication almost always re-draft their first attempt. Many people have their work re-drafted by others as well. I do. In my work, everything I write (including this) is re-written after I've thought about it and read it over. Quite often it's re-written because of the comments or suggestions of other people who have read the first version. It's still **my** work if I make the changes. Sometimes, however, it's re-drafted **for** me — but then my writing isn't being assessed by the Examination Board's markers. Thank goodness! I'm glad to say. Under those conditions it wouldn't really be my own work, anyway. I wouldn't want to claim the credit for it: for that matter, I wouldn't want to take the blame for it either.

The writing that you do over the course will sometimes be about what you have been reading, either in the class or privately, and sometimes it will be writing of stories, reports, of your own experiences (personal writing), poems, articles and so on. Some of it will be re-drafted, some not. It is important for you to know from the beginning of the course that this material is potentially valuable and should be kept carefully, using some kind of storage system. Almost certainly, your teacher will have arranged for such a system to store your work so that it does not get lost, and along with that there will be some means of labelling and identifying your various pieces of work so that you will know exactly what you have done and kept. There will also be a way of recording what you have done by using some kind of checklist: this will help you to see at a glance what you have done and what you still have to do. These arrangements are essential for you and for your teacher, and will become very important towards the end of the course when you and your teacher have to decide which pieces are to go into your official Folio to be sent to the Examination Board. It's not possible to describe exactly how the system will work for you, because it's up to each school or English department to work out their own system. The Examination Board doesn't lay down rules about the details of how it is to be done; just that it should be done. There is more detail on your official Folio in Chapter 4 and you should read and understand all the requirements there when you come to it.

All you need to know just now is that you will be keeping your written work (not every single scrap of paper, though) in some kind of storage, perhaps a folder, or loose-leaf book or in a cupboard space in the school, where it's safe and sound. Think of it as your **big Folio**; from this you and your teacher will later make the selection of pieces of writing that will go in to the Examination Board; that is your **specified Folio**.

All the details about that are dealt with in the **Folio** section, and you will see there what the specified folio looks like.

9. Coursework

I have referred several times to coursework or classwork but have not elaborated on the importance of this part of Standard Grade. Although, as promised, much more detail will be found in the section on **The Folio**, you ought to learn something about exactly how valuable it is to you that coursework is being assessed now. Before Standard Grade the work you did in class in English, your coursework, was certainly assessed by your teachers and it figured in your school reports and in other assessments made in your school, but didn't count in national assessment by the Examination Board. At Ordinary Grade, for example, and in the Highers before they were recently revised, the grade you got on your certificate was the result of what you did on the day of the examination, and that was that. Now, your classwork is taken into account as well as what you do in the examinations.

There are several ways in which what you do in class helps to decide the final award you are given at the end of the two years of your course at Standard Grade. They have to do with:

(i) Talking

(ii) Estimates

(iii) The Folio

(iv) Appeals.

I do hope that you won't really need to be involved in the last of these, but here is some brief information one each of the four things listed above, to let you see how the work of the course is very important at Standard Grade.

(i) *Talking*

During the whole of the two years of the course you will be talking. It is not punishable! Far from it ... your teacher will expect you to talk; to her or him; to the other people in your class, and also quite often to all sorts of people who are not in your class at all. Sometimes you will be provided with an obvious opportunity to talk — for example, by being asked to speak to the whole class on some subject you have chosen and thought about, such as your outstanding collection of valuable pop group posters (!), or about how you became interested in Chinese cooking, or whatever. Most of the time, however, you will not find it so obvious. The talk will be 'contextualized'. Again, that is not something that is painful or unpleasant for you; it simply means that most of the talking you are expected to do will be **in context** — it will arise quite naturally from the work the class is doing. Rather like that part of *Kes* where Billy Casper suddenly finds himself talking to the whole class and his teacher, Mr. Farthing, about how he found and then trained his kestrel. Strictly by the way, if you ever find yourself writing about *Kes*, spell 'kestrel' this way; there **may** well be another kind of bird called a 'kestral', but it seems that the slightest mention of it sends examiners into fits of uncontrollable rage.

Your teacher will be talking to you, listening to you, even eavesdropping on you — and assessing you. Your talk activities will have a purpose and your performance can be graded. Talking matters. Don't fall into the trap of thinking or saying, "No, we didn't do any work that period; we were just talking." If reading and writing are work, talking is work, too.

You already know that it counts for one third of the value of your certificate. You also now know that it is part of the coursework and is assessed by your teacher. More later on this.

(ii) *Estimates*

For Reading and Writing, your teacher gives the Examination Board an estimate grade of what the school thinks you should gain at the end of the course and the examinations. These estimates are based on the evidence your teacher has of your ability. That evidence is the work you have done in class. Though the two estimates are also based on how well the school thinks you might do in the examinations in Reading and Writing, the coursework obviously affects what these estimates are going to be. The important part played by estimates is that the Examination Board uses the estimates to help in arriving at your final award on the certificate, and, more importantly, they almost always work to your benefit. So again, through estimates, coursework counts.

(iii) *The Folio*

At the risk of becoming boring by mentioning the Folio again, I shall only remind you the Folio is **entirely coursework** in Reading and Writing. When you send it in for marking, it accounts for one third of the total possible marks for the Final Award.

(iv) *Appeals*

Despite what you may think or have heard, the Scottish Examination Board (SEB), which runs the examinations at Standard Grade, is a humane and kind organisation which tries always to make sure that every candidate in an examination has his or her work assessed fairly and does not suffer any disadvantage that would produce a wrong assessment. For this reason, the school's estimates can be used to determine your award, and, in certain circumstances, your school is allowed to 'appeal' against the award you have been given. Without going into detail about this, mainly because **you** cannot appeal (the school makes the appeal) and therefore you don't need to know the details, there is a system that makes sure that not only what you did on the day of the exam is taken into account. Unlike many other Examination Boards, the SEB will look at other evidence of your ability and performance. If I asked you to guess what that other evidence is, you wouldn't have too much difficulty in coming up with the answer. Yes, your coursework!

So, what you now know is that what you do in reading, writing and in talking during the course all has a direct and measurable effect on what kind of an award you will get at the end. It certainly does not depend only on what you do in the examination room.

10. External Examinations

This sub-section will be quite short. It deals with the second-last of the items on the list of features of Standard Grade in this section on information to help you to survive the course: so keep on reading!

When I use the word "survive" here and "survival" in the title of the book, it doesn't mean that you should be thinking of the course as the same as a disaster, the kind of event we think of when we hear the word 'survivor' — often somebody lucky enough to have escaped when others did not. No: think of it in the way we use it in connection with a **survival course** — training designed to help people to cope with difficult situations they are likely to be involved in later.

The Standard Grade course comes to an end with the external examinations. These are run by the SEB, not by the school. This is why they are called external — connected with the outside; in this case from outside the school.

There are two of them. One in Writing and one in Reading and you will sit them in early May or late April of your Fourth Year. Full details of what is in them you will find in Chapter 5 on *The External Examinations*.

Though these two exams are set and marked by the SEB and are thus completely external, don't forget that your Folio of coursework, though written in school, will also be externally assessed — that is, will not be marked in the school but sent off to be marked at the SEB. The jargon term for this arrangement is "internally generated and externally assessed" or "externally-assessed coursework".

11. The Certificate

At last, the final item of information and explanation! You should now know quite a lot about Standard Grade if you have been reading carefully so far. You can relax: there won't be any questions afterwards about what you've read. But what follows in the rest of the book will make better sense if you have read and understood the information about these 11 points. Each of them is picked up and dealt with more fully later. I have indicated which section of the book deals with which point as I referred to them. You must have noticed quite a few references to the Folio, the Examination, etc.

You can see a specimen of the certificate issued to those who gain an award at Standard Grade (Chapter 9). Actually, you'll probably notice that it's headed "Scottish Certificate of Education" and is not only for Standard, but also covers Ordinary and Higher Grades — and that it's out of date.

The certificate **you** receive will cover only Standard Grade and any subjects you sat and passed at Ordinary Grade. You don't take Higher until Fifth Year so there won't be any mention of that, nor will there be any mention of Listening on the certificate. There used to be an examination in Listening, but it was dropped in 1988, so you have missed it. No doubt you are sorry about that.

The only important thing to note at this stage of information is that if you

1. attend the course and complete the work,

2. submit a Folio to the SEB,

3. sit the exams in Reading and Writing,

you will get a certificate. That guarantee isn't offered at Ordinary Grade or at Higher Grade. In those exams you get one only if you pass the exam.

That's not what happens at Standard Grade: it has nothing to do with passing or failing. The certificate is designed to show what you have done and how well you have done it. The numbers after each element and subject connect with the grades available from 1 – 7 and the grades are directly connected with (or related to) the so-called GRADE RELATED CRITERIA (GRC). They tell whoever looks at your certificate exactly what you can do. GRC are very important for you, and they are described in a separate section of the book — Chapter 8.

Well, those are the basic things you should know about Standard Grade, but of course there's a lot more; it's a very large subject. Now we must look in detail at all those things that have been mentioned in this information section.

We start with a chapter each on the Folio, then the Examinations, then Talking.

> In these chapters there are references to the PURPOSES and the GRC. I have left the informaton on these important matters till later (Chapters 7 and 8) so that you can look them up when you need them for REFERENCE.

CHAPTER 4

THE FOLIO OF COURSEWORK

If you've already started a Standard Grade course in English, even though it might be only at the beginning of third year (S3), you have probably already heard of the Folio. Even if you haven't begun the course, and have read only this far in this book you will have heard the Folio mentioned quite a few times.

The Folio is one of the other obvious things that make Standard Grade English different from some other subjects, but very different from 'O' Grade English or Higher English (until very recently). It is an area that is not all that familiar to anyone, including your teachers. The first time these arrangements applied was in 1989, so not all teachers or pupils know everything about the Folio yet.

The Folio (the word comes from the Italian, meaning a leaf, but now meaning a large sheet of paper folded once to make two **leaves**), is the name given to the container (and its contents) submitted to the SEB by each pupil who hopes to gain an award at Standard Grade.

The very first thing to know about the Folio is that if you don't send one in to the Board you cannot get an **overall** award for English at all. Even though you sit the external exams in Reading and Writing and perform brilliantly you cannot gain an overall award: the certificate you would get would not show any final grade for English. The only thing that could be on it would be a grade for Talking. The reason for this is that, as I explained in the General Information section at the beginning of this book (Chapter 1), is that the grades for Reading and Writing are made up of half for the Folio and half for the two exam papers. What I am now emphasizing is that the **two** halves have to be present to be added together, Folio and exams. If one or the other is missing no adding takes place and you get **nothing** for Reading or for Writing. The same would apply if you sent in your Folio and decided not to bother sitting the exams. (If you missed the exam through illness or if your Folio was lost in a fire at the school, for example, the Board would make special arrangements for that, of course).

The next thing about the Folio is that it has to be sent in by your school at the correct time. That means that **your** Folio has to be completed in good time for the school to be able to have it at the SEB at the right time. There really isn't any way in which the school or the Board can do much for you if your Folio isn't available for assessment at the time the assessment (marking) is being done. National examinations and the arrangements for marking your work aren't at all like the arrangements your teacher can make for you and your class. There simply have to be clear rules and they have to be kept.

The third important thing about the Folio has to do with the contents — your work. You already know that the Folio should contain a sample of your best work, and that that sample is **specified**. In other words, what you have to send in is particular kinds of work for which there are clear rules. It simply has to be right. Most of the responsibility for getting it right is **your own**, not your teacher's, though he or she will advise you, naturally. You should not simply leave things all to your teacher, especially in the matter of the Folio, if for no other reason than that your teacher will have up to 30 pupils to deal with in making sure that your Folios are right — and that's only your class. In many schools, teachers will have more than one class doing Standard Grade. Though all teachers will check and remind you about your Folio, remember that you will have had two years of the course to produce enough work to choose from. It's your work, and you have some say in what should go into your Folio. You are the one whose work is being assessed. It's you who will be gaining the award for the work you've done and submitted.

Let me remind you here of the diagram (on page 8) showing how the value of the Folio fits into the whole scheme of things in both coursework and assessment. Since, over the whole examination, half of the value of Reading and also half of the value of Writing comes from the Folio, and since you already know that Reading and Writing together make up two-thirds of the total value, it doesn't take a mathematical genius to work out that the Folio is also worth one third of the total value of your Standard Grade award.

If you have read Chapter 2 you also know that the Folio is the odd part of Standard Grade English; it contains only coursework, but it is assessed externally — that is, by the SEB. What is assessed by the Board's markers is a specified body of coursework; that means that the Board has laid down a **specification** — a detailed list of what is required — and nothing else will do. The reason for this is that no arrangements have been made to mark anything other than what is specified, so coursework that doesn't fit the requirements cannot be assessed. That could lead to no final award on your certificate. So let's get it right.

We should look now at what you have to do to make sure that your Folio is in order when you come to the end of the course and the school is prepared to send it in to the Board. Surely it would be a pity to get it wrong after two years of coursework leading up to this point. As you now know what would be the result, it would be fair to realise that calling it a pity is a pretty mild way of looking at it; more of a disaster really.

The work you submit is meant to represent the coursework you have done and to show the best you can do in particular kinds of work.

It is a sample of your finished, polished, redrafted writing. Most of it will have been done in fourth year, but some of it could have come from units that you dealt with in third year, if it was particularly good. You'll notice that I said it was meant to be a **sample**; that is, the work in the Folio is meant to be chosen by you and your teacher from a (much) larger collection of pieces of work done over the whole two years of the course. What goes into your Folio is **not** meant to be the **only** pieces you have done in that time. This is another way of saying that you do not spend your time producing pieces tailor-made to go into your Folio. That would be allowing the course to be run by the examination system. The classic case of the tail wagging the dog. Your teacher will be well aware of that particular danger and will avoid it. No, the Folio contains your best work in each of the categories of the specification. We'll come to that in a moment.

You have probably figured out that you can't know what is your best work until you have produced other work with which you can compare it, and can then decide what is good and what isn't, and that can only really be decided towards the end of the course. Correct. Except that you will be able to recognise many pieces as good and therefore likely to come up later for consideration once you have a larger collection of pieces. This all means that apart from the most important business of producing work, you will have to have an arrangement for storing it safely until it is needed for possible selection — when you pick your team, if you like. The arrangements for this are up to individual English departments in the schools, and your school will have made suitable arrangements. There may be special cupboards or filing cabinets for each class using a particular English room, or the work may all be stored in folders in the English base. Some schools change teachers from S3 to S4 and so transfers would have to be made, too, of all the work. Whatever system the school uses, it's unlikely that they will allow much of the finished work to go out of the school. You can see why. It's absolutely essential that nobody's work gets lost before it's needed for sending in to the SEB. Your school will probably also have made careful arrangements for storing your other work in some kind of folder or file so that you can get access to it when you need it to work on it further. Sometimes this "work in progress" will be in transit between school and home and elsewhere, because you will not necessarily be drafting your early versions of pieces of writing in the classroom. You can easily guess who is responsible for it then. At the same time you should also see that you have a lot of responsibility for keeping your folder and your work in good order. Some schools will have a contents or checklist system so that you and your teacher know exactly what's supposed to be there and what stage it's at. It would be easy for you to design such a list and use it if you find that your school has not produced one for you.

> **I have something important to say about this matter of working at home or elsewhere when we come to look at the third page of the FOLIO OF COURSEWORK which is printed a little further on (page 52).**

You can probably now see that it's important that all your work should be carefully looked after and returned for storage. If you consider **yourself** much more responsible for its safekeeping than you may have felt about your jotters or whatever earlier in your school career, then you will be much more likely to come well out of the Standard Grade course.

Folio Contents: The Specification

The Folio your school will send in for you to the SEB in April of your fourth year will contain five pieces of work selected by you and your teacher from the body of work you have produced in S3 and S4 over the course, with most of it coming from the fourth year, almost certainly.

The five pieces will include:

two pieces of Writing

three pieces of (extended written responses to) Reading.

(At the end of this chapter on the Folio you will find a sample Folio made up of examples of the kinds of Writing and Reading referred to here. The various items are also graded to give you an idea of the standard described in the chapter on GRC [Chapter 8].)

We have to look in more detail at each of these items, so first;

Writing

Two pieces,

(a) **One** must be transactional/discursive
and

(b) **One** must be expressive/imaginative.

Explanations are required.

(a) Transactional/discursive writing is the kind of writing where, first of all, we are dealing with the real world rather than with the world of literature. *Transactional* writing is the kind of writing that is used to convey (factual) information. *Discursive* writing is the kind of writing used to express ideas in an orderly and formal way in writing. So, in the Folio, **one** of your two pieces of writing must be of one or other of these kinds — transactional or discursive. When you come to Chapter 7 on PURPOSES, you'll find that the first piece of writing is connected with the first two purposes of Writing.

(b) The other of the two pieces of Writing must be expressive/imaginative writing. These kinds of writing deal with your own personal world and with the world of literature. *Expressive* writing deals with your own (real) experiences and feelings — what you have done or experienced and how you react to things and events. *Imaginative* writing, as its name makes clear, is to do with the world of imagination. The kind of writing expected from you here is in one of the forms of literature, for example, a short story, a poem, a dramatisation, a letter (but not a 'business' letter!). This second piece of Writing is connected with the other two purposes of Writing listed in the chapter on PURPOSES (Chapter 7).

So, as you will see, all your writing will have a clear purpose, and the task you are given to carry out (or sometimes set yourself) should always have a clear connection with one of the main purposes.

Reading

Before going on, let me try to sort out a possible confusion. When we talk here of *Reading* we are really of course talking about pieces of work that are written down. They are **about** Reading. We can give other people information and opinions about our reading only by writing about it or talking about it. So the

Reading pieces will actually be written down in the Folio and I'll talk about them as the 'Reading pieces'. Clear?

The requirements for Reading are much more complicated than those for Writing, **and you should read this part very carefully** and regard it as a reference source. It is full of exclusions — what you cannot do if you have done something else already. First then,

> **three** pieces of work, all of them extended responses to Reading. (Close Reading [interpretation-type work] responses are not acceptable at all here).

Of the three,

> the **first two** must be critical evaluations (see page 136 for an explanation of this) each of a different form of literature. That means that you must write about (criticize and evaluate) first, say, a prose text (novel, short story, biography) and **then** either a poetic or dramatic text (either a poem or a play).

> The **third** piece can now (and only now) be any one of:

> (i) **another** critical evaluation of any form of literature, prose, poetry or drama even if you have already written about that form already

>   **OR**

> (ii) a critical evaluation of a media text (film, radio or television programme(s))

>   **OR**

> (iii) an imaginative response (explanation, see page 137) to a literary text.

> **Each piece of Reading you include in your Folio should deal with a separate text.**

> **Note also that "prose is regarded as a single genre". This means that if one of your pieces is about, say, a novel, you must not include as your other critical evaluation a piece on other forms of prose, e.g., the short story, the essay, the biography, unless you have a third critical evaluation on poetry or drama.**

I did say that this part was complicated and that you should use it as a reference source. I mean by that that you might not find it easy to carry this information about in your head, and that you should come and look it up or check when you need the information.

Further information/advice . . .

There's no way of avoiding using certain words connected with Standard Grade English (especially in the Folio). It's really best that you should use them once you've understood what they mean. It will make life easier for you and your teacher if you do.

You should certainly learn and understand what is meant by 'text' and 'critical evaluation' and 'imaginative response' because they will turn up quite often in talking about your Folio, and there probably will be quite a lot of talk about your Folio. "Text" first. The word can mean here (in the Folio specification and also in the GRC — Chapter 8) a book, or a poem, or a part of a book, or a script or play, or a film or TV programme, a short story, or a section of a novel or a whole novel. What defines it is the fact that it has been selected for study and criticism as a whole thing, an entity. This does not mean that you will always in the course have to write about a whole novel or whole play or whatever. If that was so, it would be difficult to write about any of the works you were studying until you had completed them. That would make the writing parts of many units impossible to deal with. Your teacher will want you to write about and talk about various things you are reading as you proceed from the earliest stages of the work.

The difference is that in the pieces you include in your Folio, the Examiners will expect you to make clear that you have read whole texts, not just bits of any work. So, although it's in order to produce a 'critical evaluation' of say, the last scene of *Death of a Salesman*, the Examiner will want to know how that scene relates to the whole play.

In responding to a text — that simply means writing about something you have read — in the Reading part of the Folio you can produce one of two kinds of writing: the critical evaluation or the imaginative response. These two kinds of writing about your reading are explained in the chapter on the GRC (pages 136 – 137). It's important that you understand what is meant by these if you are to have a full understanding of what you are trying to produce in the way of work from which you can later select your best to include in your Folio. Remember that the Folio contains only samples of your best work of different kinds, and the specification that you have just been reading in this chapter simply tells you what kinds, and how many. You should refer to the list in the table on page 44 or to the illustration of the Folio Flyleaf on page 51.

Length of Folio Pieces

You probably have someone in your class (maybe it's even yourself) who, whenever your teacher asks you to do a piece of writing, immediately asks, "How long is it to be, Miss?" What that question often means is, "How short can I make it? How little can I get away with?" Mostly, however, it's a genuine question: the pupil is asking **what length is appropriate to the purpose of this writing** . . . in other words, asking, "For this kind of writing, as part of the task, what length is suitable? **Is** there a suitable length?" Often there is, but equally often it can't be stated **exactly**. Usually, rough guidance as to length is what is offered: that is what the SEB has done, too. The rule always is that the length of any piece of work in the Folio (or anywhere else for that matter) is decided by the purpose of the writing. For example, you might include a one-page set of instructions and a ten-page illustrated autobiography (this is slightly exaggerated!). As long as the length fits what you are trying to do, it's fine. If it's far too short or far too long, it will be self-penalizing. If a piece of writing is too long, what we mean by that is that it contains much unnecessary material: if it's too short we mean that it doesn't contain enough material. Either way we are saying that it doesn't achieve its purpose. The writing does not manage to deal properly or adequately with what the writer intended or was trying to do.

The **suggested** lengths of pieces of work are given below. Remember, there are no penalties for pieces that are longer or shorter than the **suggested** length, generally speaking, but there is the **minimum** length of 100 words for Reading at Foundation level. You can take it that any piece of prose should be of that length, at least. In Writing, the same minimum length is **suggested**, but Poetry for example could be much shorter. The examiners are simply suggesting that there should always in the Folio be enough there for them to be able to form some clear ideas of what you can do, so that they can assesss what you offer. It's only common sense.

FOLIO PIECES: SEB GENERAL GUIDANCE ON LENGTH	
Writing	*Reading*
Foundation 100 words minimum **suggested**	*Foundation* 100 words minimum **required**
General "Appropriate to purpose"	*General* 300 – 800 words
Credit Normal maximum 800 words	*Credit* Normal maximum 800 words

Literature and Media

You will have noticed a distinction in the Reading specification between a 'literary text' and a 'media text'. The difference is simple: 'literary' here means printed book text — prose, poetry or drama — and 'media' here means film, radio or television programme(s). Notice carefully **two** things about the use of media texts if you intend to include them in your Folio.

1.   'Media' texts do **not** include the printed word for Standard Grade purposes in Reading, so evaluations of (writing about) newspapers or magazines in the Folio are not acceptable.

2.   You may include a piece about the media only if

     (a)   it is a critical evaluation

     (b)   you already have **two** critical evaluations of **literary** texts in your Folio.

N.B. "Imaginative Responses" to media texts are **not acceptable**. You may not offer, for example, a diary of a character in a film you have studied. You may be doing this kind of writing in class, and that's fine, but **don't** include it in your Folio.

Summary

So, using the words of the specification, your Folio could be made up in the following ways:

Writing — 2 pieces	Reading — 3 pieces

1. Transactional/discursive
 	
2. Expressive/imaginative
	1. Critical Evaluation
	2. Critical Evaluation
	    (both of literary texts)
	3. Another Critical
	    Evaluation — Literary
	    OR
	    Critical Evaluation —
	        Media text
	    OR
	    Imaginative Response —
	        Literary text (**not** Media)

	(a) 100 words minimum required (b) 3 different **texts** (c) 2 different **genres** (Forms of literature) (d) No close reading
CANDIDATE DECLARATION TEACHER DECLARATION	

Folio: Labelling of Pieces

I have tried to make clear for you how important the **purpose** of any piece of writing is to its success . . . how you should always know clearly what the writing is **for**: how your teacher will set you tasks that are intended to help you to meet one or more of the purposes.

It should be obvious that the person who 'marks' your work (usually your teacher(s), but for your Folio, the Board's Examiners) has to know the purpose, too. If they don't know what you were trying to do, how could they really know whether you have succeeded or not?

For this reason, each piece of work in your Folio should have a note or label of some kind telling the examiner what the purpose was, and what exactly was the task you were given, or chose for yourself. Your school will have arranged some system for this, and it will probably use the kind of label suggested by the Board, though not necessarily. It may be a similar label designed in the school, and your teacher will possibly supply them. It's a good idea to use this system of labelling your work, not just when you are assembling your Folio for sending in, but on every piece of work you start during the course. Any one of those pieces might turn out to be one that you will want to re-draft and later include in the Folio; you won't decide that till later on. One label does for the whole set of drafts and re-drafts of any one piece, so it doesn't really involve labelling every scrap of paper.

The labels suggested by the Board are attached to the 'sample folio' at the end of this chapter.

Folio: Format of Pieces of Work: Declaration

Immediately after this section you'll find an illustration of the Board's official *Folio of Coursework*. On the third page of the form (page 52), you will see three things that I have kept back till now. They are all important. The first is the **Declaration** by you that the work is your own: the second is about the use of word processors; the third is your teacher's **Declaration**.

In that order, then:

Your own work

I have said quite a lot about re-drafting earlier on. You know that the Folio pieces are to be your best, polished work. In the Folio supplied by the Board (see page 52) there is a place for you to sign a declaration that the work is your own. Because you sign that statement, it becomes possible for some of the work to be finished, following teacher guidance, outwith the classroom. Clearly it must not be done by others, nor should you be 'helped' by parents or other well-meaning persons. You are placed on trust in this matter. In addition, however, the Board will check your Folio work against your exam work. If fraud were discovered it could lead to the cancellation of your certificate — and not just in English.

The Board has not laid down fixed rules about exactly what support is permitted. It really isn't possible to be definite about when the work is yours and where the clear line is that means that there has been too much intervention

45

by someone else, so what follows can only be broad advice to keep you on the right side of the line.

You have to rely on your teacher's professional judgement always. When you draft a piece of writing, there are in it many areas that could probably be improved. Some things are obvious to yourself or to any reader. Usually these are superficial, that is, right there on the surface of the piece; things like the spelling and punctuation, the kind of things the Press gets all worked up about whenever they want to complain about the state of education. There are much more important things in any piece of writing than these. Matters like the understanding of the language structure which is shown by the writer, the structure of the composition, the effective use of paragraphing and sentence formation, of linguistic and literary devices, and so on. These are some of the things you are actually learning about in the course, and you learn them by using them in your writing under your teacher's guidance. Neither you nor they will probably use language of the kind I used above (deliberately, to make this point), but that is not important or necessary.

If you remember that your teacher's 'marking' is part of the process of teaching and part of formative assessment, you will understand how far your teacher is able to go when 'marking' a piece of work that is to go into your Folio to be assessed as your own work. They cannot write in to your work the correct version of something you have mis-spelled or mis-punctuated and invite you to copy it out. They will, however, indicate to you in matters of spelling and punctuation and similar 'surface errors' that there is something wrong in this or that **area** of your writing, and it will be your job to go and find out what, and change it for a better version. Since no-one could just mark on the page when dealing with deeper and more important matters to do with structure, syntax, style, tone, and the like, your teacher will be able to tell you about how to make improvements, and this will be a gradual process of teaching.

When you learn and change, then the work is your own. If someone else intervenes and makes changes for you that you do not understand and could therefore not have done by yourself, then that is false and pointless, and if you sign work like that intending to send it to the Board, it is fraud.

It's as well to remember that work like this will be recognised by the examiners when they compare it with your other work.

While we are dealing with a section entitled *Your Own Work*, we must also give some attention to an area that could cause you endless difficulty. It could also cost you your certificate if you got it wrong. This danger could be entitled *Not Your Own Work*. I would like here to introduce you to another new word, and I'm spelling it out for you in capital letters — PLAGIARISM. It has nothing to do with 'plague', but its effects could be just as deadly to the life of your Folio. Plagiarism is the same as theft . . . it actually comes from a word that means 'plunder' or 'kidnap'. It is the theft of someone else's work followed by the pretence that it is yours.

Where the SEB finds plagiarism, it can result in the cancellation of a certificate: that could include all the subjects on it.

It is not acceptable to send in pieces in your Folio that have been copied, or largely copied, from someone else's work, whether that someone else is a classmate or an author whose work you have read.

Where this crime presents problems is particularly in the Folio in the "conveying of information" purpose. If the information is factual then it is probably very tempting to copy it directly from another source: a reference work in the school library, for example. **Do not do this**. There is a world of a difference between, on the one hand, seeking information, learning it, and conveying it on paper in your own words, and, on the other hand, simply copying it directly. If you think about it for only a moment, you will see that what the Board is assessing is your **writing** — the **way you write** what you have to say. If you copy from a book there is nothing of yours there to assess, and that is exactly the value that will be put upon it — nothing.

Remember, anyway, that a piece like that will jump out of the page as being obviously different from your other pieces, and there's no way of hiding it from the examiners.

Standard Grade is about you being given proper assessment of what you can do with time for re-drafting and thinking and with the kind of legitimate support that has been described.

So don't be tempted to copy. When it's discovered, if collusion is involved (people acting together and agreeing to the copying) both the copier and the copied would suffer the same penalty.

Word Processing

Your work may be handwritten or typed or done on a word processor. The first two present no problem. There are no 'extra marks' for typed work as opposed to handwritten. They are marked in the same way. Handwritten work is entirely acceptable, and if you can't type well or use the word processor, then don't waste you time doing it that way.

If you use a word processor, the same applies. Most word processors, however, have software that checks spelling, punctuation, etc., **automatically** and corrects it. **You are not allowed to use such software**. You are expected to use the word processor like a typewriter, except, of course, that you can make changes and corrections to the draft on the VDU screen before you print, but these changes are the kind that **you** make manually. You sign a declaration to say that this is what you have done. Again, your work in the Folio will be compared with the work you do in the exam. Though the examiners will expect the work in your Folio to be rather better than what you do in the exam because you've been able to re-draft it and take more time over it generally, it is surprising how the quality of your work especially in using language shows through.

You can take it for granted that word processed Folios will be checked against your exam answers.

Teacher Declaration

The third thing in this group of three is also a check on the authenticity of your work. You may be getting the impression that the SEB doesn't trust you too much. That's not really true. You can see why everything about this part of the examination has to be carefully checked. It would never do for people to be given certificates which they didn't deserve. It's not only that **their** certificates would be worthless, but that they would make people doubt the value of all the other certificates gained by other people — and don't forget that one of those other people will be you.

Your teacher will sign your Folio to say that "to the best of my knowledge" it is your own. Your teacher knows what your work looks like and how it looks when you have re-drafted it properly. No self-respecting teacher is going to sign for work that doesn't seem to be your own work. If the declaration isn't signed, then the Board will want to know why, and will investigate — so that is the other check on the authenticity of your work.

So be warned!

The Folio of Coursework Flyleaf

Nothing to do with flies!

During the year you are to sit the exam in Standard Grade English (your fourth year), the SEB will send to your school enough copies of the 4-page form which follows this (page 4 is blank, so only pages 1 – 3 are re-printed here). There will be one for every candidate, including you. This is the actual folio: 2 leaves to contain the specified coursework to be sent to the Board by 31st March.

FOR OFFICIAL USE

PRESENTING CENTRE No.	SUBJECT No.	LEVEL	PAPER No.	MARKER'S No.
	0860		FOLIO	

SCOTTISH CERTIFICATE OF EDUCATION

1989

ENGLISH

STANDARD GRADE

FOLIO OF COURSEWORK

The Folio should be submitted to the Board not later than 31 March 1989.

FILL IN THESE PARTICULARS

Full Name of Presenting Centre . . . .
(including name of town)

First Name, Initial(s) of other/middle name(s)	*Surname*	*Date of Birth*

FOR OFFICIAL USE

WRITING		READING		
W1	W2	R1	R2	R3

FINAL GRADE	FINAL GRADE

FOLIO CHECKLIST

WRITING   (✓)   (✓)

W 1 Transactional/   ☐   **Either** To convey information   ☐
         Discursive   **Or**   To deploy ideas, expound,
                                           argue & evaluate   ☐

W 2 Expressive/   ☐   **Either** To describe personal experience, ☐
         Imaginative   express feelings and reactions
                               Or   To employ specific literary forms ☐

READING

		(✓) Poetry	(✓) Drama	(✓) Prose	(✓) Media	Name of Text
R 1	Critical evaluation	☐	☐	☐		_____
R 2	Critical evaluation	☐	☐	☐		_____
R 3	Critical evaluation	☐	☐	☐	☐	_____
	OR					
	Imaginative response	☐	☐	☐		_____

N.B. **These notes relate to Reading only.**

(a) Each piece should deal with a <u>different</u> text.

(b) The two critical evaluations must each be of a different genre. (For the purposes of assessment, Prose, whether novel, short story or non-fiction, will be regarded as a single genre.) The further critical evaluation or imaginative response may <u>then</u> relate to any genre.

(c) Interpretations/Close Reading answers are <u>not</u> acceptable.

(d) Selected pieces should be at least 100 words in length.

(e) An imaginative response may be presented more appropriately as evidence of Writing. Reference to the GRC for both Writing and Imaginative Responses to Literature would help decisions in this regard.

(f) Responses to Media must be critical evaluations.

SCOTTISH CERTIFICATE OF EDUCATION

ENGLISH ON THE STANDARD GRADE 1989

FOLIO OF COURSEWORK

DECLARATION FORM

This form is to be completed by the teacher and candidate responsible for this Folio of coursework.

Candidate declaration

The enclosed pieces are my own work. In any of my work produced using a word processor, I have not used any software to improve my spelling, punctuation or style.

Candidate responsible . . . .

Date . . . .

Teacher declaration

To the best of my knowledge this Folio comprises work which is the candidate's own.

Teacher responsible . . . .

Date . . . .

Scottish Examination Board
Ironmills Road
DALKEITH
Midlothian
EH22 1LE

The form contains all the necessary information as a reminder of the specification. We can now deal with it quickly. You can check the form against each item of information and advice earlier in this chapter. We don't need to spend any time on the cover page apart from noting that you will complete it with your name, school, etc., before it is returned by your school to the Board in March. Making up and checking Folios takes quite a lot of time for the school to complete, so you can expect your teacher to give you a date **earlier** than that to complete and hand in your Folio, so that they can have some time to make sure it's right and that all the forms that go with it can be filled in too. You just simply must not be late. Remember — no Folio: no overall award!

The second page is the one that really matters. It is a checklist of the items included in the Folio. When the required item is added, then the box for it can be ticked off. This page is designed to help pupils and teachers by making it impossible to include the wrong items — well, almost impossible. No doubt some people will find a way! Since there are quite a few different ways in which a Folio can be made up because of the range of options it is essential to understand the basic requirements explained earlier in this chapter.

The third page contains only the two important declarations signed by you and by your teacher. Why they are important and why they must be signed is explained already earlier in this chapter.

Sample Folio

On the next page is a sample Folio, to let you see what it might look like, complete with checklist to identify the items. The sample Folio is made up of items written by a number of pupils. Yours, of course, would all be written by one pupil — you.

Notice that the tasks (except the one on *Billy Liar*) are detailed and the purposes clear; and that the grades the Board would award for work like this have been entered on the front cover and then aggregated to give a single grade for (Folio) Writing and one for (Folio) Reading. These would later be added to the grades for Writing and Reading which this candidate, Various S. Pupils, got in the two exams.

To make them easier to read, the various pieces of work have been set up in type instead of being left in the original handwriting. The spelling, punctuation, etc., has been left as it was originally. No doubt you'll spot the mistakes! Note the good points, too, though.

FOR OFFICIAL USE

PRESENTING CENTRE No.	SUBJECT No. 0860	LEVEL	PAPER No. FOLIO	MARKER'S No.

SCOTTISH CERTIFICATE OF EDUCATION

1989

ENGLISH

STANDARD GRADE

FOLIO OF COURSEWORK

The Folio should be submitted to the Board not later than 31 March 1989.

FILL IN THESE PARTICULARS

Full Name of Presenting Centre **Stirlingbridge Academy, Blairlogie.** . . .
(including name of town)

First Name, Initial(s) of   *Surname*   *Date of Birth*
other/middle   name(s)

Various S.	Pupils	11 : 5 : 73

FOR OFFICIAL USE

WRITING		READING		
W1	W2	R1	R2	R3
2	2	4	6	2

FINAL GRADE	FINAL GRADE
2	4

FOLIO CHECKLIST

WRITING

		☑			☑
W 1	Transactional/ Discursive	☑	**Either**	To convey information	☑
			Or	To deploy ideas, expound, argue & evaluate	☐
W 2	Expressive/ Imaginative	☑	**Either**	To describe personal experience, express feelings and reactions	☑
			Or	To employ specific literary forms	☐

READING

		☑ Poetry	☑ Drama	☑ Prose	☑ Media	Name of Text
R 1	Critical evaluation	☑	☐	☐		*Streemin/Rythm*
R 2	Critical evaluation	☐	☑	☐		*Billy Liar*
R 3	Critical evaluation	☐	☐	☑	☐	*The Great Gatsby*
	OR					
	Imaginative response	☐	☐	☐		

N.B. **These Notes relate to Reading only.**

(a) Each piece should deal with a <u>different</u> text.

(b) The two critical evaluations must each be of a <u>different</u> genre. (For the purposes of assessment, Prose, whether novel, short story or non-fiction, will be regarded as a single genre.) The further critical evaluation or imaginative response may <u>then</u> relate to any genre.

(c) Interpretations/Close Reading answers are <u>not</u> acceptable.

(d) Selected pieces should be at least 100 words in length.

(e) An imaginative response may be presented more appropriately as evidence of Writing. Reference to the GRC for both Writing and Imaginative Responses to Literature would help decisions in this regard.

(f) Responses to Media must be critical evaluations.

WRITING

SCHOOL *Stirlingbridge Academy*

Name of Candidate *Various S. Pupils*   Date of Birth *11/5/73*

MAIN PURPOSE (✓)

W 1 Transactional ☑

To convey information ☑   *A REAL HOBBY*

To deploy ideas etc ☐

To describe personal experience etc ☐

W 2 Expressive ☐

To employ spec. lit. forms ☐ (Specify ....)

Detail of Task set:

If you have a hobby, write about it and use the suggestions which we have discussed to help you get your information organised clearly.

A REAL HOBBY

Modelling is my favourite hobby. To do this successfully you must have a lot of patience. To start with, a knife, cement and tweezers are a must. Paint brushes, paint and a damp cloth are also necessary.

Paint comes in many assorted colours; brands and sizes. The most common brands are "Airfix' and 'Humbrol'. 'Airfix' comes in matt or gloss and is generally quick drying. 'Humbrol' takes around six hours to completely dry and also comes in matt or gloss. To help find out which colour is which, and whether it is matt or gloss, a standard code is used. On the lid of the tin is a number (colour) and the letter 'M' or 'G'. This makes it easier if you know what you want as all you have to do is ask for 'M10' for matt white, or 'M6' for black.

Picking the actual kit is a bigger problem as there are very many brands and designs to chose from. 'Airfix', 'Humbrol', 'Revell', 'Matchbox' are just a few. I always tend to go for the better brands (see above) as less-known brands tend to have shoddy workmanship. A kit catalouge is available on request for a nominal fee.

On the side of the box is certain information which tells you what paint is needed, and what scale is used. In most cases the scale is 1:72, and different series. (I.E. series 1 is pretty small and ideal for beginners.) The series number is also given in code. CO3–7894 is the code number for the design, the O3 standing for series three.

When you have chosen a model you have to see if it's what you desire. Should you buy a car, a 'plane or a ship? If a car, what model? Pre-1914 or modern? British or foriegn?

Building the model is the next step. Armed with paints, glue, knife, etc., and plenty of paper you choose a suitable place. Then, placing the newspaper over the entire area you can proceed.

Usually after opening the box you will see the plans. These

are usually very precise and clear-cut. Various symbols are used, to glue, not to glue, to decide which piece is best fitted.

It is better to paint little pieces before assembly begins, then following the plans to commence to build the model. A model can take between thirty minutes and three weeks, depending on how carefully you do it. After assembly is finished, painting commences.

Masking tape comes in handy for camouflage, and many books are useful for this purpose. Once it is painted and the decals placed on, the model gives a sense of pleasure.

Once one is made you get better by practice.

After your first model is made a whole new world is opened up. Tanks, vehicles, trains, you name it, you can build it. Hours of enjoyment are introduced whilst you get better.

In short you improve your technique and have fun at the same time. And it dosen't make a dent in your pocket money.

WRITING

SCHOOL   *Stirlingbridge Academy*

Name of Candidate   *Various S. Pupils*   Date of Birth   *11/5/73*

MAIN PURPOSE   (√)

W 1   Transactional   ☐

To convey information   ☐   **MOVING HOUSE**

To deploy ideas etc   ☐

W 2   Expressive   ☑

To describe personal experience etc   ☑

To employ spec. lit. forms   ☐ (Specify   ....)

Detail of Task set:

Write about your earliest memory, happy or sad, showing

clearly how you felt at the time.

MOVING HOUSE

When the van arrived for the furniture I was outside watching, through the second space in the fence, the dogs I loved to play with as they were the same size as me.

I decided to go inside so I hauled myself onto my feet, with the help of the fence, waved good-bye to the dogs and slowly dragged my small feet, with their new shoes, inside. I could not see the point in dressing up just to go to a new house that I did not even want to go to!

Inside everything was bare and lonley. There was nothing on the carpets and my favourite cupboard door was standing wide open showing how empty it looked with no food on the shelves.

By the time I was ready to leave, after staring at my empty room for half an hour, all the furniture and my rabbit were packed safely in the van. My dad shouted at my mum saying everything was packed and they were ready to leave. My mum took my hand and lead me downstairs. As we descended I clutched my favourite teddy and my mum's hand as hard as I could. When we reached the bottom my mum picked up the keys for the last time and led me outside. I looked up to see my mum smiling happppily. My dad came out of the house and closed the big friendly green door I had known for all of my four years. The tears slowly crept down my cheeks as my parents dragged me to the car their large hands engulfing my small ones.

My father drove away as I sat staring out of the window crying, watching the scenery fly by. The new house was not far away but a lot bigger. We reached it quickly. My dad lifted me out of the car and carried me to the ugly, ghostly white door! The door swung open and the whole house seemed as though it wanted to swallow me up. I sat in a corner while everyone ran around trying to sort it all out. The house was large and ghostly with nothing anywhere. I decided to stay in my small corner behind the front door and watched the faces of the workmen peering at me, towering above me and then leaving to go on with their jobs.

Very slowly everything fell into place and I decided it did not look quite as horrible as it had to start with. It was late and "it had been a long tiring day for a four year old girl" as mum always said, so I scrambled to my feet and went looking for them (mum + dad). My mum was in a big room with a huge glass door at one end and a huge window at the other end. I tugged hard at her skirt. Her big round eyes loomed at me then she smiled, picked me up and carried me and my teddy up to bed. I fell asleep and dreamt of the dog we were hoping to buy. At least I had something to look forward to.

SCHOOL   *Stirlingbridge Academy*

Name of Candidate   *Various S. Pupils*   Date of Birth   *11/5/73*

(✓)

Poetry ✓

Drama ☐

Prose ☐

Media ☐

(✓)

Critical response ✓

Imaginative response ☐

Name of Text and Author:

Streemin — McGough

Rythm — Crichton Smith

Detail of Task set:

Explain what the two poems are about, what they have in common, and how the poets use language to express the boys' personalities. For which boy do you have more sympathy and why?

The two poems I have been studing are "streemin" by Roger McGough and "Rythm" by Ian Crichton Smith.

"Streemin" is told by a pupil who, because he is in the bottom stream at school, thinks he is unintelligent. However he observes that in life it doesn't matter if one is clever or not. He feels that being labelled stupid is unfair.

"Rhythm" is told by a pupil who is sitting in a English classroom looking out of a window and seeing a brick wall. He thinks that he could "smack" a ball against it but "Old Jerry" his English teacher is going on about words like English teachers do, when he slides into a daydream about scoring a goal against his English teacher. "He runs up kicks the ball, the crowd is roaring. Old Jerry dives the wrong way and a goal!" "I feel great in my gold and purpel strip straight from the wash." This boy may not be good as "old Jerry" at English but "old Jerry" wont be as good as him at football. The poems have a lot in common like both are about school pupils who are not good at their work. The pupils are narrating each poem i.e. telling their stories directly to the reader. The pupils are both poor spellers i.e. 'Ryme', 'Purpel'. Lots of deliberate spelling mistakes by the poets in the poem. Their speech is incorrect as well i.e. "arnt reely fair" "I'm in the bottom streme" "They dunno how it is". Both pupils think it is "unfair" they should be classified as "thik" and both boys dislike school.

The poems have differences too, like the boy in "Rythm" is good at football but the boy in "Streemin" is a failure.

The boy in "Rythm" focusses his antagonism on his English teacher "old Jerry". The boy in "Streemin" thinks that school is unfair. "Rythm" describes the imaginery football match. "Streemin" gives the boy's opinion. "Rythm" is easier to understand because it gives you more detail and tells you more about the person. In "Streemin" it tells you about the boy but not in detail he doesn't describe his feelings and he doesn't describe what he is good at e.g. "football", "Art".

The poet uses languages to describe boy's personality. Words deliberately miss-spelt e.g. "streemin" "Rythm" "ryme" and "dunno".

The boy in "Rythm" is more relaxed to what he is saying, the boy in "Streemin" just says words to describe him. The boy I prefer is the boy in "Rythm" because he adimits that he is daft but he also makes out he is not completely daft because he says he is good at football. The reson I dont prefere the boy in Streemin is because he says he is daft and thats that and he dosn't try to help himself.

SCHOOL   *Stirlingbridge Academy*

Name of Candidate   *Various S. Pupils*   Date of Birth   *11/5/73*

(√)   (√)

Critical response   ☑

Poetry ☐

Imaginative response ☐

Drama ☑

Prose ☐   Name of Text and Author:

                        Billy Liar — Waterhouse

Media ☐

Detail of Task set:

Response to the play.

C

The story was set in yorkshire in the late 1960s. It was about Billy fisher who was always get into mix up's. He was engaged to two girls. He didn't like the job he had. He was a clerk for Shadrack & Duxburg. He cheated the petty cash and postage money. He was always arguing with his father at home and while arguing with his father his grandmother took a fit.

Billy was always lying to Barbara, his girlfriend. The other girl who he was engaged to was rita. They both shared the ring. He also made up dreams about him self. He was offered a job with comeiden Danny Boon, But was turned down. Life was a mess for Billy.

Barbara was a up tight sort of girl. She was always eating oranges and going on aboat when they get married. Then one night at a dance the girls find out what he had Been up to. Then Billy meets Liz and decide to go to London and get married but Billy doesn't go.

I liked watching the film because you could see what was happening and you could see what kind of conditions he had to work in. You could also see what the people looked like.

READING

SCHOOL   *Stirlingbridge Academy*

Name of Candidate   *Various S. Pupils*   Date of Birth   *11/5/73*

(✓)   (✓)

Critical response   ☑

Poetry ☐   Imaginative response ☐

Drama ☐

Prose ☑   Name of Text and Author:
                                  Great Gatsby — Fitzgerald
Media ☐

Detail of Task set:

Choose a novel in which there is conflict of wills or ideals between

two of the main characters. Examine the nature of the conflict and

explain why you felt sympathy with one or other of the two, or

with both, or neither, and show how the conflict was resolved

in a way that was, or was not, satisfactory to you.

In F. Scott Fitzgerald's novel "The Great Gatsby" two of the main characters, Jay Gatsby and Nick Carraway, the narrator, have different ideals.

Jay Gatsby is the complete opposite of Nick. He is a self-made, wealthy American who owns a huge mansion in West Egg. Gatsby lives solely for Daisy, his first and last love — his whole life revolves around her and she is the reason why he has made so much money. Gatsby believes in "The American Dream" — he thinks that money is the way to his happiness. To accumulate all his wealth he has worked on the black market; his "professions" including boot-legger and gambler. Gatsby's dream is to relive his past with Daisy Buchanan, now a wife and mother. She is built up as a complete fantasy image and eventually we find that she cannot measure up to Gatsby's expectations.

In contrast, Nick Carraway is an unassuming and modest protagonist. He has extremely high morals and, in the novel, he disapproves of many of the characters. Because Nick acts as narrator, we see the main part of the novel through his eyes which gives a sometimes critical view of others. In the novel Nick can be seen as the norm. and unconciously we compare the other characters to him. He stands as the average man — a normal character who has his flaws.

As Nick himself said, "I disapproved of Gatsby from beginning to end." However, it can also be said that Nick admired and respected Gatsby. Nick did not fully understand why Gatsby was so obsessed with his dream but he kept his thoughts to himself instead of disillusioning Gatsby. Nick was not at all wealthy and his ideas on happiness were in complete contrast to Gatsby.

We, as readers, feel sympathy for Gatsby because, even from the very beginning, Gatsby is seen as a loner. He holds huge parties which are attended by thousands of wealthy people but none of them are actually very close friends. He looks to Nick for friendship and Nick is willing to give it back for he, too, is able to sympathise with Gatsby.

Sympathy is heightened for Gatsby when he is murdered. He fails to succeed in his dream and suddenly has to face reality. His life is cut short when he is mistaken for someone else and shot dead. In his death, Gatsby dies alone — he is betrayed by the people he knows, especially Daisy for whom he did everything. Gatsby's funeral is a sad affair with only three people present. Nick stands by him to the end.

The minor conflict of ideals between Gatsby and Nick at the end is resolved when we see Gatsby's death. Nick no longer criticises Gatsby about his eternal search for happiness through money. Instead he greatly sympathises with Gatsby, finding himself "on Gatsby's side, and alone". The conflict is now resolved in that Nick now sees Gatsby in a new light.

Although it is very traumatic, it seems appropriate that Gatsby should die at the end because it has been seen that Gatsby can no longer fulfill his life-long dream (Daisy) and so, instead of letting an extremely sad Gatsby continue his life, Fitzgerald opts to have Gatsby killed to end his miserable life. This, for me, is a far more suitable ending as it ties together everything very neatly as opposed to leaving Gatsby to live on as the novel draws to a close.

SCOTTISH CERTIFICATE OF EDUCATION

ENGLISH ON THE STANDARD GRADE 1989

FOLIO OF COURSEWORK

DECLARATION FORM

This form is to be completed by the teacher and candidate responsible for this Folio of coursework.

Candidate declaration

The enclosed pieces are my own work. In any of my work produced using a word processor, I have not used any software to improve my spelling, punctuation or style.

Candidate responsible *Various S. Pupils* . . . .

Date *20/3/89* . . . . . .

Teacher declaration

To the best of my knowledge this Folio comprises work which is the candidate's own.

Teacher responsible *M.Y. Teacher* . . . .

Date *20/3/89* . . . . . .

Scottish Examination Board
Ironmills Road
DALKEITH
Midlothian
EH22 1LE

70

That completes what you need to know about the Folio, one-third of the whole examination. Now on to the next one-third — the external examinations.

PHEW

!

CHAPTER 5

THE EXTERNAL EXAMINATIONS

In Section 10 of Chapter 3 (page 32), the basic information chapter, all that was said about the external examinations was:

  (i) there are two: Reading and Writing,
 (ii) they take place in late April/early May each year,
(iii) they are set by the Scottish Examination Board.

If you have been reading systematically through the book so far (congratulations, and you're near the end now) you will know that the two written examinations make up a further one-third of the total value of your award.

What you achieve in the Reading paper is added to the "Reading" component of your Folio: what you gain in the Writing paper is added to what you got for the "Writing" component of your Folio. These give your grades for Reading and Writing and all together add up to two-thirds of the total award for English.

Writing

We'll look first at the external exam in Writing. It isn't anything like as complicated as the one in Reading. One of the reasons for this is that in the Writing exam you are writing and it is Writing that is being assessed: in the Reading exam you are writing but it is Reading that is being assessed. If that sounds puzzling you should go back and read what was said about the four modes of language ... the expressive and the receptive modes. The writing that you do in the exam is assessed directly by grading; there is no conversion from marks to be done as you'll see there is for Reading. Another thing that makes the Writing exam more straightforward is that you are pretty familiar with the kind of things that you are asked to do in the exam. In its simplest form, it is really just asking you to choose a topic and write about it, keeping clearly in mind the purpose of the writing.

It is easy to see how the Writing paper does this by looking now at the sample of part of the paper printed here. I haven't printed the whole paper because once you've understood the main idea, the rest of the paper is very similar: it just offers you more choice on the day.

SCOTTISH CERTIFICATE OF EDUCATION

ENGLISH

Standard Grade

FOUNDATION, GENERAL AND CREDIT LEVELS
PAPER II — TEST OF WRITING

Wednesday, 27th April — 9.30 a.m. to 10.45 a.m.

READ THIS FIRST

1. Inside this booklet, there are pictures and words. Use them to help you when you are thinking what to write about.

   - The photographs are on one side of the page.
   - What you have to do is set out on the facing page.
   - The assignments are numbered.
   - There are 17 altogether for you to choose from.
   - Choose only **ONE** numbered assignment.

2. Study all the material and think about all the possibilities.
   Decide which assignment you are going to write about.

   - Plan what you are going to write.
   - Use the photographs and other suggestions as much as you need.
   - It is important to make sure that you are doing what you have been asked to do.
   - You may give your work a title, if you wish.

3. If you redraft your work, your changes should be made clearly.

4. Read and check your work before you hand it in.

5. You **MUST** write in the margin the number of the **ONE** assignment you have chosen.

FIRST

Look at the photograph on the opposite page.

You can see the telephone engineers' little tents and van outside the shops.

NEXT

Quite ordinary?

- Imagine what might **really** be going on.

Think of the difficulties.

WHAT YOU HAVE TO WRITE

1. Write the story of what was **really** happening and how it was all uncovered.

   OR

2. Imagine that you are the owner of either the 'Pop-in Stores' or the 'General Wolfe' or of the 'Tattoo Artist'.

   Write a letter describing your difficulties and complaining about the upset.

75

FIRST

Look at the photograph on the opposite page.

A ruined building sits among the trees at the foot of a mountain. There is no-one about.

NEXT

- take a moment to remember how you felt as a child in a place like this.
- free, in complete privacy, with no-one watching you, alone.

WHAT YOU HAVE TO WRITE

3. Describe how you feel about being alone. It may be something you fear, or what you prefer.

    OR

4. 'It was very nearly dark when I saw the castle.
    I knew that there was nowhere else that I could spend the night ...'
    Continue the story suggested by this beginning.

    OR

5. There is an old building near where you live.

    One plan is to demolish it; the other plan is to restore it as a hotel.

    Write a letter to your local newspaper giving your views.

The first thing to note is that there is a question paper but you do the writing in a separate booklet, not in a question/answer booklet with spaces for the answers. That alone makes it much more like the kind of writing that you will have been doing in the class.

The second thing to note is that although the paper contains **quite** a lot to read, it is all set out in the most readable step-by-step way for you. The reason for that is connected with the next point.

The Writing paper is the same for everyone who sits Standard Grade. There are no different levels. For this reason the reading task is set within reach of all readers at whatever level of ability.

The front cover gives all the information and the instructions that are the same every year: the other instructions for the particular year are inside the booklet.

The things to note that will be the same every year are:

1.   The exam is the same one for everyone at Standard Grade and you can gain any Grade from grade 1 to grade 6.

2.   The exam lasts for one and a quarter hours.

3.   There are photographs, illustrations and words as a stimulus to writing (that simply means that you are given ideas to write about).

4.   There is a large number (usually about 15 to 20) of assignments (tasks) and you choose only ONE.

5.   The purpose of the writing will be made clear to you.

6.   You may redraft your work if you wish to, and if you have time.

There is a little more to be said below about some of these items when we have a look at the sample pages of the inside of the booklet of pictures and assignments.

The sample inside pages you can see are obviously going to be different in the details from year to year, but there are some things which will always be the same. They are:

1.   The instructions will always be clearly set out.

2. There will be choices of the **kind** of writing you can do.

3. These choices will cover the various PURPOSES of writing (described in Chapter 7 on Purposes).

4. The choices available to you will allow you to write so that you can meet the demands of the GRC for Writing.

Because, as I've already said, the kind of writing you are asked to do in this part of the exam is familiar to you, and because I said that this chapter would be short, there isn't a lot more to be said about it. There is some advice, though, that can be given about your choice and about how you do your writing.

Though the job you are facing in the Writing exam is more familiar than, say, the Reading exam, there are one or two things you have to be careful about. Let's start with the choices you could make.

Choice of Assignment

The chapter on *Purposes* (Chapter 7) and the one on *The Folio* explain that there are these two broad types of writing — the kind that conveys information and the kind that is imaginative or personal. The exam will offer assignments of both of these kinds of writing and they will not be difficult for you to recognise. Once you have recognised them and made your choice, you must keep in mind the purpose of that kind of writing.

Long before you come to sit the exam you will have found out during the course which kind of writing you like best and can do best, and that will certainly influence your choice.

You can see from the sample pages quite clearly that there are chances for you to write imaginatively or about your own personal experience, or to write in order to convey information or argue a case — the same categories of writing that you had to produce for your Folio about a month before you sit the exam. Though you can't tell this by looking at the small sample I have given you, you should also know that this choice of the kind of writing is generally available for each of the separate assignments grouped around a particular picture or other stimulus in the exam paper. This means of course that you should read the whole paper before deciding which one to choose.

Though you might well know in advance the **kind** of writing you are going to do, it doesn't follow that the first assignment you come to of that kind is going to suit you perfectly. It's quite likely that there will be an even better one further on in the paper. For example, if you have decided that you really want to write about a personal experience and find that there is on the first page an assignment that invites you to do that, but is connected with a picture of, say, a football crowd, and the last thing on earth you want to write about is an experience at a football match, either because you hated it or because you've never been to one, then obviously you're not stuck with that particular personal writing assignment.

You read further on in the question paper booklet until you find another personal writing task that's connected with a picture or word stimulus that you can, as they say, 'relate to'. Maybe it's a scene at an airport and there's an invitation to write about a holiday that went wrong or was very enjoyable. That might be a much better choice for you if you had just had such an experience. You're still choosing personal writing, but not stuck with a subject that you either don't know much about or don't like very much. This is very important, make no mistake about it.

You are certain to produce much better work when you are writing about something that you know about and which really interests you. So look for such an assignment and make your choice carefully — and when you have done that make sure that you understand the purpose of that particular piece of writing and keep to it. You won't be offered a choice of an assignment or topic that simply says "Write in any way you choose about any old thing you can think of". You wouldn't be asked by your teacher to do that kind of thing in the class or for your Folio. All your writing will have a purpose and the task will be clear to both you and your teacher.

Re-drafting

On the front page of the exam paper printed earlier in this section you can see that you may re-draft your work. You have to be careful about this in the exam, because the situation is not the same as what you will have got used to during the course. Re-drafting your work isn't just writing it out neatly a second time. In the class you will have had time to think about what you have written and you will have had opportunities to discuss it with your teacher and/or with others in your class or group. Re-drafting a single piece could be spread over quite a long time — several periods or a few days or even longer, with time in between to reconsider how you want to say what you think, and set it down carefully for the final version.

In the exam, things are very different. The main difference is, of course, the time available to you to do the writing: the other main difference is that you will not have the chance to ask anyone else what they think about it. Your friendly teacher will be shut out of the exam room, and there will be only the other candidates and the Board's Invigilators who supervise the exam. You are not allowed to consult any of them about your writing. You really are on your own in this. Not as bad as it might appear at first glance, however. By the time you come to sit the exam and are faced with perhaps re-drafting your work you will have had two years' experience of writing and re-drafting and you will be much better at it than you were when you first came into third year.

So although we know that the kind of writing you are doing in the exam is fairly familiar to you, the conditions are a bit different from those of the classroom. It's why the writing exam has jokingly been called 'writing under stress' — only jokingly, though. There is quite a lot of support to be found in the question paper, as I've said, and you're quite a competent writer at this stage.

In re-drafting anything you write in the exam you do have to take account of the time available. What **not** to do is to write for an hour and then cancel it all out and attempt to write a better version in the remaining 15 minutes. You can see that that would lead to disaster in terms of a grade for your work — not likely to be a very high one for an unfinished piece of writing.

The way to proceed with re-drafting your work is to make sure that you leave enough time to re-read and re-draft and complete. There are two ways to do this and you will have learned one of them at least during your course.

You re-draft section by section as you work through the piece of writing, or you complete a first draft and then go back over the whole piece re-drafting as necessary. The second of these methods is probably the better one for **this** particular situation with its time limit. It means that you have a finished piece of work even if you run out of time ... something you should not be doing ever. The first method means that you could end up with a polished but incomplete piece of writing.

That brings us to timing.

Timing.

This is brief. Part of the job in the writing exam is to do the writing within the time set. When I referred jokingly to "writing under stress", I should have mentioned that a more respectable name for it might be "timed writing". We all know that it doesn't have much connection with the real world. We seldom have time limits set on what we write. That's not the same as having a deadline. Often we do have these. I certainly do. (The completing of this book has gone on long past the deadline: fortunately the publisher, Mr. Gibson, is very patient.)

The reason for the timing has to do with the need for a national examination that provides the same measurable chance for everybody who sits the exam. It just isn't practicable to do otherwise. The Folio gives you the chance to show what you can do when you are not working within the limits of time.

In tackling the writing exam, never think of it as a time when you sit down and write for an hour without stopping. The task has several parts and they each need time set aside for them.

Read the Instructions carefully and calmly.

Make your choice of assignment.

Think about the assignment and make a plan.

Write the first draft, keeping to the plan and/or amending it as you work on.

Read over your work carefully and thoughtfully.

Re-draft it as necessary.

Check it again.

Number it.

There is no special merit in writing a longer piece than anyone else. Most of the assignments could be very adequately covered in about two or three pages of the exam book you'll be given to write in — and the lines in it are broadly spaced apart!

This means that you might not **start** writing for a good ten minutes, and when you do it would be the planning stage rather than the actual composition. When you do start writing even then it does not mean that you should be still scribbling furiously when the Invigilator tells you to stop.

Part of the time will be spent reading what you have written, part of it re-drafting, much of it thinking and further planning, and, importantly, at the end you should make sure that you have set aside rather more than five minutes to check and correct if necessary what you have written. This is almost as important as the actual writing.

If you fix in your head the notion that when the exam comes to an end, you are either calmly and carefully reading and finally checking, or you are already finished everything, then you will have got the timing right.

We now have to look at the rather more complicated arrangements for the exam in Reading.

Reading

Like the GRC for Reading (dealt with in Chapter 8) the Reading exam is the slightly more complicated of the two elements.

By some time in the fourth year, you and your teacher will have a fair idea of the standard of work you are capable of producing, and this, broadly speaking, is a useful guide to you both as to how you should tackle the Reading exam. You'll see why.

Levels of Examination: Presentation

The external examination in Reading is offered at three levels: Foundation, General and Credit. In each of them there is a passage for close reading (like interpretation) and questions to match. Each passage and its questions is set at a level of difficulty to match the GRC for that level (described in Chapter 8 on the GRC). They are set like this to give you the chance to show what you can do in whatever level of paper you attempt. The SEB allows you to sit **either**

    (i) the Foundation paper only

OR

    (ii) the Foundation and General papers

OR

    (iii) the General and Credit papers.

Your school 'presents' you for these papers in advance (in about November of your fourth year): that is, you are entered for the level or levels at that time. This 'presentation' is based on the level or standard of your work up till then, allowing for what improvement you could make up till the time of the exam in April/May.

> **YOU SHOULD TAKE YOUR TEACHER'S ADVICE ABOUT WHICH PAPER(S) TO SIT. HE OR SHE IS THE PERSON WHO KNOWS BEST HOW TO GUIDE YOU IN THIS.**

You teacher will always present you for papers that will allow you to do your best on the day.

This is how it works. If your work in Reading seems to be mostly fitting the GRC at Foundation level, but sometimes shows the standard described by the GRC for General level you should sit FOUNDATION AND GENERAL. If you mostly seem to be doing work and achieving grades at General level with occasional Credit level performances, you should sit GENERAL AND CREDIT.

If your work is almost always at Foundation level standard, you should probably be sitting the FOUNDATION paper only, but you have nothing to lose by sitting the FOUNDATION AND GENERAL. If, at the other extreme, your work is most consistently at Credit level, you should sit GENERAL AND CREDIT. As you can see from this advice, most people will sit **General and one other level of paper**, either Foundation or Credit. There's a very good reason for this.

At any part of Standard Grade, because everything is based on GRC, **you can only get an award for what you have actually achieved**. You cannot get any award for any level you did not sit. This means that if you sat only the Credit level (you're allowed to do that — be presented for General and Credit, but on the day sit only one of them: the same for Foundation and General — but it would be very unwise to do so!) and if you did not score enough marks to gain the Credit award, you would not be given an award at General as compensation. You would drop right down to Grade 7: the same would happen to you if you sat only the General paper on the day and failed to gain enough marks for a General award; you would drop right down to Grade 7. You wouldn't be given a Foundation award.

It works the other way round, too. You cannot get a General award by

84

doing very well in the Foundation paper, or a Credit award by doing very well in the General paper if you sat only the lower level of paper in each case.

The reason for this is that the GRC say that you "can do" various things, and there has to be clear evidence that you can.

So, you should pay very careful attention to your teacher's advice both on the level of 'presentation' for Reading papers, and on what papers you should sit on the day.

Everything said so far about 'presentation levels' applies **only** to the external exams in Reading. The level at which you are presented for Reading has no effect on the grades you can achieve for your other work:

> in the Folio, both Reading and Writing
> in the external Writing exam (see previous section)
> in the Talking element (see Chapter 6).

You could gain a different grade, anything from grade 1 to grade 7 for any of the separate parts of the whole of Standard Grade English, at least in theory. In practice, most people will be a little more consistent than that and will tend to get grades that are fairly similar to each other for the various parts. Some examples will help to make this clearer; I'll give you some easy ones first.

The headings are for the various bits of Standard Grade that add together to make up the final award. You could go back and look at the diagram near the beginning of the book if you prefer pictures to words or tables of figures.

Close Reading	(Folio) Reading	Writing (Exam)	Writing (Folio)	Talking
3	3	4	4	2
∴ Reading = 3		∴ Writing = 4		Talking = 2
Final Award = 3 + 4 + 2 = 9 ÷ 3 = $\boxed{3}$				

Now a slightly more complicated mixture of grades to show you that the same arrangement works and still produces a final grade.

Close Reading	(Folio) Reading	Writing (Exam)	Writing (Folio)	Talking
3	5	5	6	2
Reading = 3 + 5 = 8 ÷ 2 = 4		Writing = 5 + 6 = 11 ÷ 2 = 5·5 = 5		2
Final Award = 4 + 5 + 2 = 11 ÷ 3 = 3·6 = $\boxed{4}$				

So, how it works is that all the sub-grades are added for each element (for example Close Reading 3 + Folio Reading 5 gives 8) find the mean (the average) by dividing by 2. The answer is 4. If the answer is not a whole number, it is rounded up to the higher of the grades on either side. In the second example, Writing 5 and Folio Writing 6 gives 11. Dividing by 2 to give the average produces 5·5. The grades on either side of 5·5 are obviously 5 and 6. Grade 5 is higher than grade 6, so the grade you get is 5. The **final** award is based on a total of 3·6. That is nearer 4 than 3, so the result is grade 4.

Once you have a grade for each element they are added and the mean is calculated in the same way. The only slight change is that since there are three elements and they are all equal in value, you divide by 3 to get the final grade for English.

You can see from the examples given that the level of paper you sit in Reading doesn't fix what grades you can get for any of the other parts of the exam. It does have an **effect** on the overall or final grade, naturally, since the highest grade you can get for Reading depends on which level of the Reading paper you took.

Reading: The Question Papers

This book isn't about how to sit the Reading exam and how to practise. Actually the work of the course is much more important and the best preparation for the exam. In the exam you should be displaying a sample of what you can do. You should never, however, think of the course as a way of practising to sit exam papers.

There is a companion book to this one called *Reading for Standard Grade English* by Ken Cunningham and published by Robert Gibson & Sons, and it will be very helpful to you in the 'how to do it' of both the Reading exam and the Reading required in the course and in the Folio.

The exam in Reading deals only with what we call Close Reading (that's why Close Reading doesn't have any place in the Folio: that deals only with Extended Responses to Reading). I've said that Close Reading is familiar to you as Interpretation: actually, it's rather more than that. You could think of it as "Super-Interpretation": what you do when you really get down to examining in close detail what you read. Reading under the microscope, if you like.

Taking an adapted version of one of the SEB's recent papers (at General level only) as an example, we can study how it works and what is expected of you. Here is part of the paper, the passage and questions. It has been reduced to half size. The actual paper size is A4 (297 cm × 210 cm).

SCOTTISH CERTIFICATE OF EDUCATION

ENGLISH

Standard Grade — GENERAL LEVEL — PAPER I

TEST OF READING

Time: 10.15 a.m. to 11.05 a.m.

Read the following passage carefully. It describes the thoughts of Malcolm, a teenage boy in his last year at secondary school, who lived in a remote village in the Western Isles of Scotland.

While you will be asked questions about particular details of the text, you should keep in mind the main ideas running through the whole passage.

When you have read it — and it will help if you read it through twice — you should go on to answer the questions. Use the spaces provided in the question/answer paper.

Try to answer all the questions

HE WAS SITTING on the peat* bank looking south. It was a fine day and the moor, spongy under his feet, was covered with heather bells: a breeze gently stirred his trousers. The sky above him was a blue inverted vase, unflawed, unscarred; and in the depths of it a skylark was singing deliriously. He
5 had a book in his hand which he wasn't reading. He was sixteen years old and it was wartime. Somewhere else guns were being fired, sailors were being drowned. Here there was no sound; no sound whatsoever except for the humming of a bee or the skylark, or the buzz of a fly. Below him, the peats were set in their black pyramids, wet, dripping and new. The peat bank
10 itself was a shiny scar among other shiny scars on the moor. He swung his legs down over the edge of the peat bank and looked down, conscious of his body. The pages of his book fluttered in the slight breeze. He looked south.

It was there she lived. He had never seen the house for it was in a different village from his own, about three miles away across the moor. He could walk
15 there in the direction of the sea and look at it, the house where she stayed, the house where she woke at morning and slept at night. His thoughts about her were pure. She was a goddess, someone out of a Greek or Roman book of legends. She walked on air. She was clothed with fire, as the poets wrote. She was so far above him that he could not aspire to her. She was sixteen
20 years old and lived in that village three miles away and he had never seen her house. But sometimes he would come out to the moor by himself and look south, to where she lived, dreaming of her. It was impossible to do other than dream about her.

What else could he do? What chance would he ever have of doing
25 anything else? He was a worm. He was a good scholar. He played football rather well. But he couldn't swim and he wasn't a fighter. He ticked off all the things he couldn't do. He knew nothing about mechanical things: he couldn't do algebra well, though he was good at geometry. In some things he was slow: in other things he was very quick. But the trouble was that what he
30 was quick at, other than football, were scholarly things, like Latin or English or geometry. He hated having to climb the roof to put the felt on it. He didn't like tarring the roof or mending fences. He was clumsy. There was no way round it. He was not suited to her. Furthermore, he was poor and he had no style. He was liable to blush, he couldn't talk to a girl. In fact, he was useless.
35 For instance, there was Ronny: he knew everything about girls. He was as much at ease with them as he was with boys, perhaps more so. He hated Ronny, envying him his grace, his sophisticated manners, his air of rich negligence. He envied him his deceptively lazy mind, his almost adult self-

* peat: a dark turf cut and stacked for use as a fuel.

88

possession, his cleverness among people, and that subtle, dangerous quality
40 in him which could turn almost to sadism. Why, he had even taken her to the
cinema a few times. He had told everyone about it. Imagine him with her in
the cinema in the darkness! Malcolm's mind spawned images of light and
dark, chocolates and oranges, white limbs and red plush seats, coquettish
glances in the night.

45   He couldn't bear it. In this summer, this last summer which ought to be
perfect and unflawed like the sky but wasn't and never would be again. He
banged his hand down savagely on the book. These wasted years of learning,
had they not left him clumsy and terrified? Staring south he thought of her,
black-haired, the blood coursing vigorously under the skin of her face which
50 had the sheen of a rare fruit. He thought of a Gaelic proverb about the
highest apple on the bough, and was miserable again because it told of her
infinite distance. She, in the schoolgirl's uniform, with her smile, her white
teeth. The yellow belt at her waist. Her voice. The look in her eyes as if she
were eternally laughing, bubbling over. And looking south he knew she was
55 there by the sea. At this moment she was there. What was she doing now?
Only to be with her would be enough. To look at her, to breathe in her
vicinity. Not even to speak if that did not suit her.

[END OF PASSAGE]

G

SCOTTISH CERTIFICATE OF EDUCATION

ENGLISH

Standard Grade — GENERAL LEVEL — PAPER I

TEST OF READING

10.15 a.m. to 11.05 a.m.

Fill in these boxes, then turn over the page.

Full name of school or college

Town

Christian Name/First Name, Initial(s) (of other/middle name(s)))   *Surname*

Date of Birth
  Day   *Month*   *Year*

*Number of seat occupied
at examination*

Write your answers in the spaces provided.

1. The second sentence tells us it was a fine day. Write down **two** words from the first paragraph which tells us that there were no clouds in the sky.

   (i) [   ]   (ii) [   ]

   | 2 | ■ | 0 |

2. What is unusual about the use of the word "depths" (line 4)?

   _____

   _____

   _____

   | 2 | ■ | 0 |

3. Look again at the sentence which begins: "Here there was no sound . . ." (line 7).

   | 2 | 1 | 0 |

   (i) What sort of atmosphere is the writer trying to create in this sentence

   _____

   and

   (ii) How does he use the sentence before it to emphasise this atmosphere?

   _____

   _____

   _____

4. Explain, as fully as you can, why the writer should describe the peat banks as "scars on the moor" (line 10).

   _____

   _____

   | 2 | 1 | 0 |

   [   ]

   PAGE
   TOTAL

5. "It was there she lived." (line 13)

Why do you think he has never walked to her house?

_____

_____   2 ■ 0

6. "She was a goddess . . ." (line 17).

(a) **Write down** three things from the rest of this paragraph which fit
in with the idea of "a goddess".   2 1 (

(i) _____

(ii) _____

(iii) _____

(b) What **two** things do the words, "She was a goddess", tell us about
the boy's feelings towards her?   2 1 ■

(i) _____

(ii) _____

7. In the third paragraph the boy makes a mental list of the things he is
good at and those at which he is not so good. Look at the table below.
Put a (✓) beside the things he is good at, and a cross (×) beside
those at which he is not so good.   2 ■

algebra	
swimming	
English	
playing football	
tarring roofs	
geometry	

8. *(a)* Why does the boy make this mental list of the things he is good at?

_____

_____

(b) What is the problem about most of the things he is good at?
Explain this as fully as you can.

_____

_____

_____

. Look again at the paragraph describing Ronny (lines 35 – 44).

(a) Which of the following words best describes the boy's attitude
towards Ronny? Tick (✓) the answer you think is best.

(i)

indifferent	
admiring	
jealous	
contemptuous	
resentful	

(b) Explain in your own words, as fully as you can, why he feels this way
about Ronny.

_____

_____

_____

(c) **Write down** a word from this paragraph which suggests something very unpleasant about Ronny.

2 ■

(d) **Write down** a sentence from this paragraph which reads as if the boy is actually saying it aloud to himself.

_____

_____

_____

2 ■

10. "Malcolm's mind spawned images . . ." (line 42). Explain fully why "spawned" is a better word to use here than, for example, "produced".

_____

_____

_____

2 1

11. Look again at the description of the girl in the fifth paragraph (lines 45 – 57).

(a) In what way is this a very different kind of description from the one in the second paragraph? Explain as fully as you can.

_____

_____

_____

2 1

(b) **Write down** a phrase from this paragraph which reminds you of the description in the second paragraph.

_____

2 ■

2. We are told five times in the passage that the boy is looking south.
Why should the writer repeat this point so often?

_____

_____

2 1 0

3. Write a description of Malcolm as a person, based on all the
information contained in the passage.

_____

_____

_____

_____

_____

_____

2 1 0

[END OF QUESTION PAPER]

PAGE
TOTAL

TOTAL
MARK

95

The passage is chosen as suitable in difficulty of reading level for General Level, as set out in the GRC. It could in any given year be prose or poetry or drama. It could be illustrated or not. It could be longer (though not much) or shorter (though again not much shorter). It could be formal or colloquial in its style of language. In other words, there is no guarantee that the question paper that you will face on that sunny day in May will look **exactly** like this one. It will, however, be of the same standard of difficulty and will almost certainly be an interesting read.

You will most probably be sitting a paper at General Level if you have taken your teacher's advice and when you sit this paper you will either have already sat the Foundation paper earlier or you will be going on to sit the Credit Level paper immediately afterwards.

The questions that follow the passage are printed in a separate booklet with spaces for you (in the exam, that is) to write your answers. These spaces are carefully planned. They are there to give you some guidance about the kind (length) of answer expected from you. The Reading paper is **not** a test of Writing. Quite often only the briefest of answers is required — indicated by several lines, or a single line, or a box, or even a small box for a tick to be inserted in a multiple-choice question. The examiners do not expect short essays as answers. They should be full, but concise — enough to convey the clear meaning but usually without over-elaboration. When the examiner wants the answer in your own words, this will be clearly asked for in the question, or at the beginning of the paper.

The Marking System

Down the right-hand side of each page of the question paper there are three columns, as you can see. Against each question there is an indication of the mark or marks available for that question. There are two kinds of question, broadly speaking

(i)   Questions where there is an answer worth either 2 marks or 0 marks. In the columns opposite this type of question you can see the entry

$$|\,2\,|\,\blacksquare\,|\,0\,|$$

You can gain 2 marks for the right answer: no other mark is available. These questions are dichotomous, that is, capable of right or wrong only, with no partial credit.

(ii) Questions where the answer may be right, partly right, or wrong.

In the columns opposite these questions you can see the entry

| 2 | 1 | 0 |

You can gain 2 marks for the right (or full) answer, 1 mark for a partly correct (or less full) answer, and, of course, 0 marks for a wrong or unacceptable answer.

The columns of marks are set out like this to let you know the kind of answer expected and its value, and also to allow the Board's markers to record your marks accurately and clearly. They circle the mark awarded you for your answer. That's why there is a 'black box' in the 'dichotomous' questions. It prevents the marker from accidentally awarding partial credit in that kind of question.

You will have noticed that all the questions are therefore of the same **maximum** value as each other and the difference between them is in the way you gain credit for answering them: all or nothing for the first kind; all, part or nothing for the second. This is one of the ways in which the examiners distinguish between the upper and lower grade at each level of the exam.

How Marks Become Grades

These Close Reading papers are the only part of Standard Grade English where your work is assessed in marks. All the other parts are directly graded — each of the Folio pieces, the Writing exam, the Talking. Close Reading can't be graded directly. The separate questions have to be 'marked', the total score added up and then converted to a grade so that it can be added to the other grades (for Talking and the Folio and Writing) to arrive at your final award for English. How this is done is not simple, but it is important to know about it.

When the question paper is constructed, the passage and the questions are arranged to allow you to 'demonstrate performance' (show what you can do) at the level attempted, and they are matched with the purposes described in Chapter 7. The examiners calculate what scores of marks in that paper are needed to get the upper and lower grades. These are 'cut-off scores'. The cut-off scores for a particular paper will not be the same as for all other papers. The reason for this is that it is actually a percentage of the number of marks in the paper, and that number will vary from paper to paper and year to year. Also,

D

because the examiners check the paper not only before but also after the exam the final cut-off score is decided after the exam has been taken. There are quite a lot of things that affect it, but **as a general rule**, to gain the upper grade at any level, you will have to score about 70% of the marks available, and to gain the lower grade at any level you would have to score about 40% of the marks. This percentage figure remains constant from year to year and across all papers. It is the total marks that vary and other things that affect the paper after the exam. These have got to do with the simple fact that pupils who sit exams don't always do what the examiners expected, and the examiners have to take account of this to make the exam fair for all who sat it.

So, if you had a General level paper with 30 questions, the maximum marks available would be 60 (each question worth 2 marks). The cut-off score for grade 3 would be 70% of 60, which is 42; the cut-off score for grade 4 would be 40% of 60, which is 24. Notice that you do not have to get **all** the marks to get the grade. The examiners realise that though strictly speaking you should get all the questions right because the GRC say that someone who gets that grade can do all of the things mentioned, the exam samples and tests these several times over, and the people who sit exams are human beings who make mistakes and are not always consistent. The 70% rule allows for this.

You can get a **total** mark by any combination of marks for answers to 2 – 0 questions and 2 1 0 questions. For example, you could get 21 questions worth 2 marks each, or 12 questions worth 2 marks and 18 questions worth 1 mark. Notice too that you would have to get at least 12 2-mark answers before you could gain the upper award in this example. That is quite a high proportion of the total number of questions, 12 out of 30, especially when you then have to get 18 other marks. If you dropped even one of those marks you would gain the lower award, not the higher. So although you can gain the higher or lower award by different combinations of answers, you don't get either of these awards for nothing.

The cut-off score, then, is affected by a number of factors but you can take it that the principle is always the same. It makes sure that those who gain the awards do so on the basis of what they can do, as described by the GRC. The percentages I have been talking about have nothing whatever to do with the number of people who sit the exams. There is no percentage of **candidates** who gain awards at any level. If you can do what the GRC demand, you get the award regardless of what other people do.

CHAPTER 6

TALKING

Chapter 8 contains quite a lot of information about Talking GRC. This chapter gives you some advice about dealing with talk in the classroom.

You know that the talking you do in the two years of coursework will be assessed and will be worth one-third of the 'marks' for your final award in English. Also you will see from the chapter on the GRC that there will be two kinds of talk to be assessed and that they are of equal value. The difference between these two kinds of talking — Discussion and Individual Talk, is explained there too, as is the place that listening has in Discussion.

As far as the exam is concerned, the main difference between Talking and the other parts of the examination is that it's the only part that is assessed internally, that is, by your class teacher.

That's the reason for this chapter being rather short. The sections on the Reading exam and the Folio, and even the one on the Writing exam are much longer because there is an exam for those parts. In Talking there isn't.

The nearest we come to an exam is that in some schools (and yours may be one of them) some of the assessment of Individual Talk will be "set up" and will maybe feel more like an exam situation. I hope that it's not all going to be like that in your school, and that your talking will be assessed as it happens naturally during the whole course, arising from the normal work of your class.

Teachers have to assess what you can do, and this has to happen more than once during the course. Your teacher will probably want to hear you in Discussion and in Individual Talk on several occasions over the two years, with most of the assessments made nearer the end of the course than at the beginning. You will probably be better at talking at the end of S4 than you were at the beginning of S3 (teaching does have an effect on you). After all, you will be being taught about talking and you will certainly be learning it by doing it, the best way. You will have quite a lot of "hands-on" experience of talking during the course. As you know, it is one of the important ways in which learning is carried forward. Talking over your ideas and opinions is one of the main ways in which you really learn about things ... or, as someone said, "I don't know what I think until I hear what I say". When you spend much of your time in the course talking to your group or teacher or class, you are learning.

Discussion especially is valuable in confirming your learning. It is not only learning about how to talk: talking certainly is one way to learn how to talk better (I don't mean elocution: I'm coming to that), but it is also how you learn about thinking both logically and imaginatively (they're not opposites): about reading, about listening, and definitely about writing. Remember that writing is the mode of language that is closest to talking. These two modes are the ones that allow you to 'express' your thoughts, ideas, opinions, information — to communicate with others.

Never underestimate the importance of talking. It is never 'just talking'. If you think that you learned to talk without any effort, you're wrong. It actually talkes an enormous amount of effort to learn what language you have by the age of five, and you learn almost everything else you know up till that age by listening and talking. You certainly didn't learn it by reading, did you? Talk and language don't just happen. If you had been born and lived in another country, say Hungary, you would know all about the problems of learning English, the language you probably take for granted; it would be just like having to learn Hungarian now. Not easy. One of the Scottish kings tried an experiment to see what the 'natural' language would be of a child who was deprived of all teaching. The child was sent to live on an island in the Forth in the care of a nurse who was deaf and dumb. The belief was that the child would probably speak Gaelic — the 'language of Heaven'. There was much surprise that it didn't in the end speak any language at all. It hadn't had anyone to teach it how to speak. Funny if it wasn't so tragic. Talking and language have to be learned.

You will be taking part in several different kinds of talk activities in your class. In Individual Talk, you might find that you are asked as part of a unit to give a talk to the whole class. Since you are the only one talking in that situation, it's the one that will feel most like the exam experience. Unlike in an exam, however, it doesn't always have to count towards your final grade for Talking. Much of the time you will be learning how to do it by practising how to do it, and the assessments that count will be made nearer the end of the course. Your earlier attempts help you and your teacher to improve your performance.

Other activities in Individual Talk will include reporting a discussion to the class, taking part in debates, either formal or informal, being a member of a panel — a group of people who answer questions from the audience. The questions, which you might or might not see beforehand, are sometimes handed in in advance and you would have time to sort out your ideas and give your opinions.

Whatever activity you carry out in talking will have a purpose and that means that your performance can be assessed.

Role-Play

The word 'performance' has been mentioned several times in this book. It just means what you do, and how well you do it. It has nothing at all to do with acting, as in a performance of a play on a stage. Which leads us to a matter that has to be cleared up.

Sometimes when you are talking, you will be asked to do it 'in role'. Your teacher will give you a task and tell you that you are, for example, one of a group of people up in a hot-air balloon. The balloon is losing height and unless you can lose weight by jettisoning someone — throwing him or her overboard — the balloon will crash and you'll all be killed. Not a very moral example, is it? For the purpose of the argument, however, we set aside the horrible idea behind it and the group is to discuss who's to go. Quite quickly, as it happens, because the balloon is losing height rapidly. You each argue in the role, from the point of view of a person who might be more valuable than another. One of you is a doctor, one a teacher, one a nuclear physicist, one a joiner and one a pop-singer. I know, I know — you've already decided who should go! Notice that you're not being asked to be a pop star or Albert Einstein or any other indentifiable person, or to impersonate that person. The point is, you don't ACT: you talk. How well you do in talking depends on how well you can talk from the point of view of such a person. It doesn't involve acting like a teacher or a pop-star. It is not a performance as on a stage. You might be able to be assessed for that kind of performance if you were to take a Standard Grade course in Drama once that subject course has been set up in your school, but not in Talking.

By the way, that kind of activity is not original. It's often called a 'balloon debate': the joke solution to the problem is that if everybody keeps on talking a lot of nonsense, it will produce so much 'hot air' that the balloon will fill up again anyway, and there won't be a problem any more.

Accent

Another area of Talking that you should be quite clear about from the start is the matter of accent. The course is not about elocution — what some people call 'speaking posh' or 'speaking proper'. That is a different matter altogether, and the GRC for Talking say nothing about it. That means that it is not being assessed at Standard Grade and has no effect on the grade you might gain. All of the talking you do will be carried out in the accent you have learned, mainly because of where you live. Accent has to do with intonation and the pronunciation mainly of vowel sounds in your normal speech. Most people have local accents, and there is nothing wrong with that. You will be expected to speak in an appropriate register, however. That simply means choosing the appropriate kind of language for the situation. Most people know how to do this and choose correctly without giving it very much thought. It's a very complicated area, this, and is easily misunderstood if you just read about it. If I say that you would know what set of language to use if you were speaking to your best friend one minute and the next you were to speak to the Queen. You would not change your **accent**, but you would want to change the **register**: you would want to be rather less familiar in speaking to the Queen, possibly more formal, and you would also think more carefully about getting your grammar correct. All you would be doing would be choosing the appropriate register.

Provided the register is appropriate and the formal rules of spoken English are applied, the accent of any one part of the country is no better nor worse than any other. So, if you come from Inverness or Galashiels or Auchtermuchty, your accent is entirely acceptable for Talking at Standard Grade. There is no need to try to speak in the accent called 'RP' — Received Pronunciation. It was modelled on the accent of part of the South-East of England and took on some **social** importance when it was adopted by the BBC when broadcasting first started. It should also be said that if you **do** speak RP — it is not really a **local** accent any more — then that is perfectly acceptable, too.

The educational world has learned that if you set out to attack and destroy people's speech, you attack their very culture, their roots. It's like insulting them and telling them that their way of life is not as good as the one with which you wish to replace it.

These comments on role-play and accent apply to both Discussion and Individual Talk.

There are some further matters connected with Individual Talk that need some comment. We have looked briefly at some forms of Individual Talk already, especially the kind where there is one speaker addressing an audience which simply listens. You should remember that occasionally the audience may be very small — a group of four or five people, or even just a single partner.

Provided that the talk is not 'interactive', as explained in the GRC chapter, your talk can be assessed as Individual Talk. For some people this is a much better way to go about it. Talking is very closely connected with your personality and if you are a person who just cannot talk when faced with a larger audience, you teacher will understand that and arrange that you can talk to a suitable smaller audience. That is acceptable. Let's hope, however, that if you go through a Standard Grade course, and especially if there has been a similar approach earlier in your school career, you will feel confident by the end of S4 to talk to anyone about anything at any time. That is what Standard Grade is hoping to achieve for you.

Illustrated Talk

If you give a talk to your class and you want to use things like OHPs, slides, diagrams or real objects to illustrate it, remember that your task is to TALK, not just to point to things, or show pictures. The audio-visual aids you use must be supporting your talk, not replacing it. The GRC deal with how you succeed in communicating by talking, so you will only be successful if the aids fit into and back up, clarify or illustrate your talk.

Demonstrating

This is very like an illustrated talk in that you might be using things to support your talk. If you remember all the time that although you are showing how something is done (mending a puncture on a bike, or sewing on a button, for example), the important thing is the communicating by talking. Simply doing the job and pointing to things won't get much credit as talking. Again, the GRC don't deal with these matters, so what you do and point at can't be assessed as far as Standard Grade English is concerned.

Using Notes

You are allowed to use notes if you are giving a talk, but the notes should be no more than headings to remind you, and you will not do well if you bury your head in them, lose eye-contact with your audience and do more reading than talking. The GRC deal with talking, and you will do **badly** if you simply read aloud. The same applies to a talk that has obviously been **memorized**. It won't even sound like a talk. It comes too close to reading aloud, and both of these have more to do with the skills expected of an actor. Since the GRC deal with talking as defined for the purposes of Standard Grade, these two forms of speaking are unacceptable for assessment — they cannot be assessed as talk and count for nothing.

By the end of the course, when you have had a chance to carry out these activities of talking on many occasions, you will be able to say what you have to say without notes, or with maybe a postcard with a few headings to remind you of the points you want to make. The thing that makes this possible is that you will know what you are talking about and that you will be clearly aware of the purpose of what you are doing.

To finish this chapter which I said would be short, a few paragraphs on some matters to do with Discussion. Some of it you already know, but there's never any harm in saying it again for emphasis.

Discussion

First, discussion is carried out by a group, and all the members of the group should contribute to the discussion. You must not sit quietly listening with your lips zipped shut. You must talk. That does not mean that you should talk just for the sake of talking. It isn't a competition to see who says most and keeps the others from talking. Quite the contrary. Somebody who did that would get a very low grade for discussion because they would actually have ruined the discussion and failed to achieve the purpose.

The purpose will be to exchange views, information, opinions, feelings and attitudes on a topic, and carry out together the task that was presented to the group. It's always a joint venture, a collaborative activity. There are no 'winners'. It is not to force others to believe or accept your point of view.

The Chair

Some discussions will have a 'chair' or chairperson (formerly chairman). This person, and it may be you, has certain additional duties in a discussion. So if it is you, you have to share out the time appropriately among those who take part. It is your job to give everyone a chance to speak, and to encourage them by asking them: to summarize what has been said both during and at the end of the discussion. Importantly, the chairperson is not just a referee or umpire. He or she must contribute views and ideas in the same way as all the others in the discussion.

Assessment

In case you are wondering how assessment of talking is carried out, and how we can be sure that it's right, a quick summary before we leave this chapter on Talking and go on to the Purposes.

Your teacher carries out continuous assessment over the course. This is done by a combination of Individual Talk and Discussion in roughly equal balance. You will see and know that talking is being assessed — most obviously when there are "set-piece" individual talks, and perhaps less obviously when your teacher sits in or eavesdrops on discussions. He or she won't sit there with a clipboard and the GRC sheet as you talk — that would probably ruin any attempt you were making — but they will use the GRC, and they will hear you in Individual Talk and Discussion several times over. Towards the end of S4, they will consult their records of the assessments they have made, and come to a single 'summative' grade — a final one summing up all the others — for Talking. That will be sent to the SEB at the same time as your Folio, in March of your Fourth Year.

Your teacher's assessment will be moderated by the SEB. That means that all teachers of English with an S4 Standard Grade class will be trained and tested by the Board so that the grades from all teachers all over the country will be using the same standard. That's very important. It's also important to know that all the teachers in your school's English Department will be using the same standard as each other.

That arrangement is made by the Board for any subject that has internal assessment. The Purposes and the GRC are the same for everyone anywhere in the country. The way they are used must be, too. So your grade (1?) for Talking should be the same as all the others, no matter whether the school is in Stirling or Stranraer or Stornoway or anywhere else, and the certificate will have the same value.

Talking of the Purposes and the GRC, the next chapters deal with them, and it's time to move on.

Sorry that this chapter stretched out more than I said it would, even when re-drafted.

CHAPTER 7

THE PURPOSES

There is a very important matter you should know about in your course, and especially in the assessment of your work that goes on for the whole two years during which you will be doing Standard Grade. This matter is one that will also be very important during the assessment at the SEB of your Folio and of the work you do in the actual written examinations at the end of the course. I have mentioned it already and promised to tell you about it further on. Well here we are further on and ready to deal with the **Purposes**.

Everything you do in all the coursework and again in the examinations will have a purpose ... while you are doing it you have to know what the purpose of the work is. Equally importantly, while your work is being assessed, the assessor (your teacher, the Board's examiners, sometimes your classmates, sometimes yourself) can only do that job properly if he or she or they know what was the purpose. They must be able to see how well you have achieved the thing you set out to do ... to fulfill the purpose.

The four modes of language — Reading, Writing, Talking and Listening — have each a number of purposes. These are what we carry out activities in the language modes **for**. **Why** we read, write, talk and listen. To try to show you how important these purposes are, I have set out this list:

the GRC are based on the purposes

the units are planned on the purposes

the courses are constructed around the purposes

the tasks and assignments set for you are aimed at the purposes

the examinations are set on the purposes

the Folio specification depends completely on the purposes

and

the assessment depends on the purposes.

That should give you a fair idea of how important the purposes are.

If they are that important to the whole structure of Standard Grade English, it's pretty obvious that you should know about them too. It is crucial for you to understand how they fit into the whole scheme of things at two important stages in your course; the first of these times is not really just one time at all. It is necessary for you to understand about the purpose every time you start work on a task or piece of work set by your teacher; so that is a time that is repeated almost every day. The other time in the course when you really have to know the place of the purposes is when you came to consider items for including in your Folio. As you can see from the list on page 44, the items that go into your Folio are "specified", and that means that the items that the Board wants from you are chosen because they match one or other of the purposes. This is explained in **great** detail in the chapter dealing with the Folio.

One of the clear ideas that comes through in Standard Grade English is that all work is going to be better if the person who has been asked to do the work has the answers to such questions about it as "Why?", and "For what or Whom?" and "How?". That applies to any single piece of work you may be faced with in English, although it appears most obviously in writing, you might think. If your teacher asks you to write a letter it is impossible to fulfill the purpose if that is **all** that you know about the task. If your teacher wanted you to write a letter to a friend describing what had happened to you yesterday when you broke your leg, but didn't tell you that, and just said "Write a letter", quite a lot could go wrong in the writing. If, without asking for any further information when you had been asked just to "Write a letter", you decided that you would write to the makers of your alarm clock complaining that it didn't work (as I had to do yesterday), this would lead to an absurd situation. There is a complete misunderstanding of what the task is; there would also therefore be a complete difference in thinking about how successful your letter was and thus it could not be sensibly assessed. Only if everybody is clear about the purpose can any work be fairly judged against the clear criteria. In case you are thinking that you only ever do work in school so that someone can mark it, it should be said that for (almost) everything we do in school or outside, we usually have a purpose. If we know what we are doing and why we are doing it, and importantly what we are doing it **for** and what we hope to achieve by doing it, the chances are that we will do it better than otherwise.

In simple language, both you and your teacher should know exactly what you are being asked to do so that, amongst other things, when the work is finished it can be properly assessed for what it is. As a matter of fact, unless you both know what the purpose is, you won't even know whether it is finished or not, nor will your teacher be able to teach you what you need to know next about it.

As I said above, each of the 'modes' of language has a set of purposes; they set out what we hope to be able to achieve in studying the language in any mode. You should know what they are, and it's a very good idea with all your work (not just your written work) to look at what you have been asked to do (or have decided to do) — the task — and try to match it against one of the purposes for the 'mode' you're working in. You'll find, of course, that some pieces of work involve more than one purpose for any particular task. When you look at the purposes listed below you should be beginning to see that there is a strong continuing linkage in what you do. Maybe a list to show the connections between the various parts of Standard Grade will help to make this clearer:

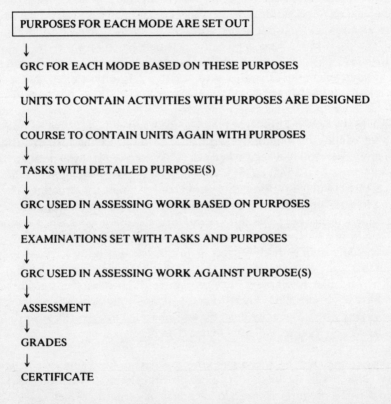

The main thing about the diagram is that the PURPOSES are in the box that connects with everything else. The exact order of the items in the list changes depending on which part of the system you are starting from: but always the PURPOSES and the GRC have important and strong connections with all the other parts.

Having said that each of the four modes has clear main purposes, I should now say that the two "expressive" modes, Writing and Talking have similar purposes, obviously, and that the two "receptive" modes, Reading and Listening do too. For that reason I have run the purposes together : not to save space, but to emphasize the connections.

The main purposes of *Writing* and *Talking* are closely related. We write and talk to:

(i) convey information

(ii) deploy ideas, expound, argue and evaluate

(iii) describe personal experience, express feelings and reactions

(iv) employ specific literary forms (for example, short story, letter or poem) (in Writing)
create particular effects (in Talking).

Naturally, in the same way that the purposes above for the "expressive" modes are closely related the main puposes of the "receptive" modes, *Reading* and *Listening* are closely related to each other. We read and listen to:

(i) gain overall impression/gist of a text (R)
gain overall impression/gist of a message (L)

(ii) obtain particular information from a text/message

(iii) grasp ideas or feelings implied in a text/message

(iv) evaluate the attitudes, assumptions and arguments expressed

(v) appreciate the writer's craft (R)
appreciate the techniques used (L)

(vi) enjoy and obtain enrichment from a text/message.

Though there are one or two words here that might not be familiar to you (for example, evaluate, deploy, expound, etc.) you can look them up or ask about them. Even without knowing those words, you can understand what the Purposes are doing here. **They set down our basic reasons for doing anything connected with English**. Whenever you or anyone else is reading, writing talking or listening, one of these main purposes is there. Because of that, we have got clear why we are doing English. Therefore your teachers can decide what to teach you, you know what you have to learn, the things your teachers ask you to do in the course are designed to teach you how to do these things and the assessment is designed to find out whether you can do them or whether you need more teaching and learning — and the GRC help to measure how well you can do them at the end of the course.

Note that I said that the GRC are based on these purposes. You can actually follow step by step through the various statements of each set of GRC (next chapter) and connect each one directly with a purpose statement listed above. Every task you undertake, both in the coursework and in the examinations should fit with one of these purposes, and sometimes with more than one. So check.

The exception is in the Listening purposes. Since listening is not being assessed **separately** the purposes for listening have been taken up in the GRC for Talking in the Discussion section. Listening is still very important, however. You can't do well in Discussion without listening to the others in the group. It is also, of course, one of the main sources of learning. Much of what you learn comes through talk, and that is why you have to listen to learn.

As we said at the beginning of this chapter, if you understand the place and the importance of the purposes in the whole system of Standard Grade English, you will be much more likely to produce a better performance all round. It will also be clearer to you each time your teacher sets you a task from one of the units you have been dealing with, what you are expected to do and this will help you to stick clearly to the purpose of what you are doing. You will also make more sense of the assessment of any of your work. You should also be able to see what the Folio specification (see Chapter 4) is doing: making sure that a sample of your work aimed at the purposes of Reading and Writing can be assessed. Again, you can now see that the external examinations contain questions and tasks that are designed to allow you to produce work based on some of the purposes of Reading and Writing. Finally, on the assessment side, you can see that the things you do in Talking and to some extent Listening are based on the purposes listed above.

Let's turn to the nitty-gritty of the GRC, long promised.

CHAPTER 8

THE GRADE RELATED CRITERIA

We come now to the Grade Related Criteria. They will be called "GRC" from now onwards. I write "they" because "criteria" is a plural: the singular is "criterion": one criterion, two criteria. It means the standard upon which a judgement or assessment may be based, a point of reference for valuing something. Those are dictionary definitions. It would probably be helpful if you think of them as the descriptions against which **your** performance is measured. That is one of the fundamental things about Standard Grade. Your work is not compared with the work of other pupils in your class or anywhere else for that matter; only against the GRC.

That is why they are central to Standard Grade. Almost everything else depends on them.

"Criterion" is a very popular name for hotels and pubs. If you have seen such a place and wondered about the name, now you know. Choosing that name means the owners are saying that this is the hotel or pub against which all the others are measured: it sets the standard.

GRC are not some kind of deadly or dangerous virus, though with a name like that you could be forgiven if you thought so. Think of them simply as **descriptions** of what a pupil can do in Writing, Talking and Reading. If you do, you will not need to bother about the awkward "jargon" name. I have tried throughout the book to avoid using any of these jargon words and have tried to use plain English wherever I can. I have had to use some of them, however, but these are either explained when they are mentioned, or become clear from the context (the other words around them and the subject under discussion). I have had to use the word "assessment" quite a lot, you'll have noticed: another word like "marking" is probably familiar because it's used in school, but it doesn't quite carry all of the meaning of "assessment".

GRC is one term that can't easily be avoided.

This is the hardest part of the book both for you, the reader and for me, the writer. I am going to try to explain and 'de-jargonize' the GRC.

Many people, and especially teachers ever since Standard Grade was started have made a lot of jokes about the amount of jargon used in connection with it.

One of the phrases that has caused much amusement (and loss of temper, too, probably) is GRC. Teachers have what could be called a love-hate relationship with GRC. One of the best jokes was accidental, as these things often are. It was on a very large road-sign beside major road-works at Bridge of Don near Aberdeen — on one of the very few days when I didn't have a camera with me. You can see a drawing of it here. GRC of course stands for **Grampian Regional Council.**

Well, GRC are not exactly inconvenient. For Standard Grade they are essential. They are a public statement of the standards required for all of the grades of award possible for each of the elements, Writing, Talking and Reading. They are used by the SEB and by your teachers to assess your work and to arrive at the grade you have achieved. They are used by all the people who are 'users' of the certificate — employers, parents, other schools, colleges, universities and so on. Most importantly for you, however, is that they can be used both by you and by your teacher as the targets for you to aim for and reach at the end of the course. During it as well.

This is because they describe the performance (what a pupil has produced) that is required for each of the grades it is possible to gain. So you can read them and find out how good your work has to be for a Credit or General or Foundation level award. You find this out by looking at the **Summary** GRC. They give you a general idea. They are printed right after this.

There is a description, as you can see, for each of the three levels, Foundation, General and Credit for Writing, Talking and Reading. "The candidate", though you may not recognise yourself, is you. In school you are a pupil, or perhaps a student: in the examinations you are always a candidate.

The Summary GRC are not at all difficult to understand, because they are written in fairly straightforward English. They are meant to be read and easily understood by you and the public at large. That is because they are intended to explain generally what the grades on the certificate mean. They **describe** but they are not used by teachers and examiners for **assessing** your work. For that we need more detail, and that means the 'extended GRC'.

SUMMARY GRC

Writing

Credit Level (grades 2, 1)

In finished work the candidate communicated meaning clearly at a first reading. Formal errors were insignificant and sentence construction was accurate. There was some distinction in ideas and language. The work demonstrated a detailed attention to the requirements of the task. Where appropriate, the candidate sustained the quality of the writing at some length.

General Level (grades 4, 3)

In finished work the candidate communicated meaning at a first reading. There were some formal lapses but sentence construction was mostly accurate. Ideas and language were on the whole adequate and the work demonstrated a reasonable attention to the requirements of the task. The candidate was able to write at a length appropriate to the task.

Foundation Level (grades 6, 5)

In finished work the candidate managed to communicate meaning largely at a first reading despite formal errors and weaknesses. The writing was limited in ideas and language, but showed a few signs of awareness of the requirements of the task. Where appropriate, the candidate was able to sustain a length of at least 100 words.

Talking

Credit Level (grades 2, 1)

In discussion and individual talk the candidate conveyed substantial and relevant ideas readily; expression was fluent. The candidate was consistently aware of the purpose and situation of the talking. In discussion close account was taken of others. In individual talk language was varied and accurate and there was little or no prompting.

General Level (grades 4, 3)

In discussion and individual talk the candidate conveyed relevant ideas adequately; expression showed some traces of variety. On the whole, the candidate was aware of the purpose and situation of the talking. In discussion account taken of others was reasonably regular. In individual talk language was generally accurate; some support was needed through prompting and questioning.

113

E

Foundation Level (grades 6, 5)

In discussion and individual talk the candidate managed to convey a few simple ideas; weaknesses in expression did not prevent communication. There were a few signs of awareness of the purpose and situation of the talking. In discussion account taken of others was intermittent. In individual talk the candidate used a limited range of language and needed substantial support through prompting and questioning.

Reading

Credit Level (grades 2, 1)

The candidate demonstrated in writing a good understanding of whole works and extracted passages. These passages went beyond what was readily understandable or related to personal interests: they sometimes featured unfamiliar, abstract ideas and complexity of structure and tone. Grasp of ideas was firm and there was sound appreciation of the author's purpose and technique. The candidate made a perceptive and developed statement of personal response to what had been read.

General Level (grades 4, 3)

The candidate demonstrated in writing a fair understanding of whole works and extracted passages. These passages were on the whole readily understandable, were mainly related to personal interests and dealt with relationships or ideas in a straightforward way. Grasp of ideas was on the whole adequate and there was appreciation of some obvious aspects of the author's purpose and technique. The candidate made a reasonably developed statement of personal response to what had been read.

Foundation Level (grades 6, 5)

The candidate demonstrated in writing some evidence of understanding whole works and extracted passages. These passages were brief and readily understandable, were related to personal interests and dealt with relationships or ideas in a straightforward way. Grasp of ideas and appreciation of the author's purpose and technique were rudimentary. The candidate showed traces of a personal response to what had been read.

THE EXTENDED GRC

When we come to the Extended GRC, that is, the more detailed versions intended to be used in assessing, things become more complicated.

First of all, there is the more specialized language, or, if you like, jargon. Jargon is, however, quite appropriate. After all, it is only a form of shorthand. Every job or profession has its own jargon, and that is unobjectionable. These Extended GRC are meant to be used by teachers and by the SEB for assessment, and that is their job. The whole purpose of this book is to let you understand as much as possible about Standard Grade: the more you know about what you are expected to be able to do (the GRC) the better you may be able to do it. The GRC are as hard to grasp as some other jargon. Take this one example from the world of sociology:

> ". . . the cognitive-affective state characterized by intrusive and obsessive fantasizing concerning reciprocity of amorant feelings by the object of the amorance".

All that can be said in one word, — | LOVE |

which is what the sociologist who used this was trying to define. No doubt it has its place and possibly other sociologists knew what he was talking about, but if one of the graffiti at the back of the bike shed at your school suddenly announced

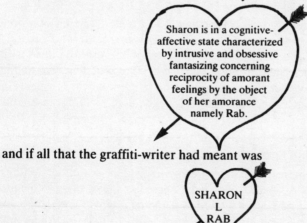

and if all that the graffiti-writer had meant was

people would be rightly surprised — and possibly puzzled. The GRC don't look as difficult as that, do they?

If we take the most straightforward set first, things will become clearer fairly quickly.

WRITING G.R.C.

	CREDIT	GENERAL	FOUNDATION
	The work displays some distinction in ideas, construction and language. This is shown by a detailed attention to the purposes of the writing task; by qualities such as knowledge, insight, imagination; and by development that is sustained. Vocabulary, paragraphing and sentence construction are accurate and varied.	The work shows a general awareness of the purposes of the writing task. It has a number of appropriate ideas and evidence of structure. Vocabulary is on the whole accurate, but lacks variety.	The work shows a few signs of appropriateness and commitment to the purposes of the writing task.
AS THE TASK REQUIRES, THE CANDIDATE CAN	convey information, selecting and highlighting what is most significant;	convey information in some kind of sequence;	convey simple information;
	marshal ideas and evidence in support of an argument; these ideas have depth and some complexity; he/she is capable of objectivity, generalisation and evaluation;	order and present ideas and opinions with an attempt at reasoning;	present ideas and opinions in concrete personal terms;
	give a succinct account of a personal experience: the writing has insight and self-awareness;	give a reasonably clear account of a personal experience with some sense of involvement;	convey the gist of a personal experience;
	express personal feelings and reactions sensitively;	express personal feelings and reactions with some attempt to go beyond bald statement;	make a bald statement of personal feelings or reactions;
	display some skill in using the conventions of a chosen literary form, and in manipulating language to achieve particular effects.	use some of the more obvious conventions of a chosen literary form, and occasionally use language to achieve particular effects.	display a rudimentary awareness of the more obvious conventions of a chosen literary form, and occasionally attempt to use language to achieve particular effects.

A combination of these qualities may be called for by any one writing task.

	CREDIT	GENERAL	FOUNDATION
INTELLIGIBILITY AND CORRECTNESS	Writing which the candidate submits as finished work communicates meaning clearly at a first reading. Sentence construction is accurate and formal errors will not be significant.	Writing which the candidate submits as finished work communicates meaning at first reading. There are some lapses in punctuation, spelling and sentence construction.	Writing which the candidate submits as finished work communicates meaning largely at first reading: however, some further reading is necessary because of obtrusive formal errors and/or structural weaknesses, including inaccurate sentence construction and poor vocabulary.

DIFFERENTIATING FACTORS	GRADE 1	GRADE 2	GRADE 3	GRADE 4	GRADE 5	GRADE 6
	The finished communication is not only clear; it is also stylish. Attention to purpose is not only detailed; it is also sensitive. Writing shows overall distinction in ideas, construction and language. Vocabulary is apt and extensive, and paragraphing and sentence construction are skilful. In these respects performance transcends the level of accuracy and variety acceptable at grade 2.	Evidence of one or more of the qualities of distinction in ideas, construction or language is present but these qualities are less well sustained and/or combined than at grade 1. In the main writing is substantial, accurate and relevant, but it lacks the insight, economy and style which characterises achievement at grade 1.	Writing is characterised by overall adequacy of communication. It conveys its meaning clearly and sentence construction and paragraphing are on the whole accurate. There is a reasonably sustained attention to purpose, and structure shows some coherence. Where appropriate there is a measure of generalisation and objectivity in reasoning.	Writing approaches the qualities of adequacy required for grade 3 but is clearly seen to be impaired in one of the following ways: there are significant inaccuracies in sentence construction, or the work is thin in appropriate ideas, or the work is weak in structure.	Writing rises a little above basic intelligibility and rudimentary attention to purpose. Formal errors and weaknesses are obtrusive but not as numerous as at grade 6. Attention to the purposes of the writing task is weak but the quality of the writer's ideas is perceptibly stronger than at grade 6.	Writing contains many formal errors and structural weaknesses but they do not overall have the effect of baffling the reader. The conveying of simple information is marked by obscurities and extraneous detail, and the presentation of ideas, opinions and personal experience is somewhat rambling and disjointed.

Writing GRC

At this point you should keep your finger at the GRC page and turn back for the various points referred to so that you can look at what you are reading about. This will make the explanation easier to understand as you go along.

The GRC for Writing are quite straightforward, apart from some of the jargon words used. You will probably have to look up some of them.

Quite a lot of what is being said in the GRC makes more complete sense when read together with the advice being given in the Folio and Examination sections earlier in the book. The 'task' mentioned will be given by your teacher if the writing is coursework, and by the Board's examiners if it's in the Writing exam. The same GRC are used to assess them. Wherever the task comes from, it will make clear what you are to do, what is expected, and it will be related to a Purpose. In other words, whatever you are asked to do, it will give you the opportunity to produce a piece of writing that can be measured/assessed against one or more of the Purposes of Writing. It's important for you to know exactly what the task is, exactly what is required. Whether you have managed to do what was required and how well you have managed are the main things used to determine the grade — how close you have come to fulfilling the demands of the GRC in making your work match the Purpose. You have already read the short chapter before this one on the Purposes for the various elements, Writing, Talking and Reading.

If it is important that you understand the task and how it is intended to help you meet the requirements of the GRC, then it is equally important that any task you are given should allow you to do that — should allow you to show how you are doing what the GRC demand in your pieces of writing.

The Writing GRC are laid out so that you can see that there is a description for each of the three levels, Credit, General and Foundation, and also below these "differentiating factors" for each of the two grades at each level: 2 and 1 at Credit; 4 and 3 and General; 6 and 5 at Foundation.

I said at the beginning of this whole chapter that starting with the more simple GRC (for Writing) would make the rest more easily understood. I hope you agree that the Writing GRC are fairly easy to follow. So easy that you might care to do a little self-assessment. You should be able to take some of your own pieces of writing and try assessing them against the Writing GRC. If you do, you can quickly see how the GRC can be used as **targets**. If you can assess your work as it is now, you will have been able to 'tick off' those areas where they match the GRC, and at the same time note where they fall down. You learn where your work should improve: not in detail, but generally. Your teacher will be able to pinpoint the same strengths and weaknesses — and go on to help you with the necessary improvements, something that cannot be done by a book.

The remaining problem with the GRC is of course that they use words to describe performance, and everyone who reads the description thinks that they know exactly what is meant — that is until two people are faced with the same piece of work and believe that it matches the GRC description exactly — except that one thinks it matches the General description and other thinks it is more of a match with the Foundation description. Obviously the words of the GRC are capable of different interpretations, and for that reason, we need examples of work which we can say are clear illustrations of the descriptions in the GRC. The SEB has provided examples of this kind for your teachers (in Reading and Writing, at least) and I have copied some of these examples as illustrations in the Folio chapter of the book, earlier on. There is a Sample Folio, with different pieces of work in it, and these pieces are given the grades the SEB would give them.

One thing to notice in using the GRC to grade a piece of work is that quite often a single piece of Writing does not match the GRC for say, Foundation level in every way: it may also show signs of General level performance. The grade it is given is the one it matches most consistently.

Later, you can check the Writing items in the Sample Folio in Chapter 4 and see why they have been graded as they have.

It should be becoming clear that there is an unbroken connection in Standard Grade between the GRC and teaching and learning.

Talking GRC

So far, not everything has been said about the place of Talking at Standard Grade. Its place in the course is very important. In the examination as a whole it is worth one-third of the whole value of your work, as I'm sure you already know if you've been reading the information presented earlier. In the course, talking comes into everything you do, not only in what are obviously the talk activities, but also in all the preparatory work connected with reading and writing.

Because of its importance in the course, Chapter 6 dealt with that. This chapter deals with the GRC only, and at this stage we are dealing with the GRC for Talking. For more details on the actual activities of Talking, read the earlier chapter, too.

TALKING (Discussion) GRC

	CREDIT	GENERAL	FOUNDATION
SUBSTANCE AND RELEVANCE OF CONTRIBUTION	Is substantial in quality and relevant to purpose of discussion. Provides a good number of relevant ideas/ responses/opinions/experiences. Supports ideas with evidence. Questions and answers relevantly.	Contributes some relevant ideas/ responses/opinions/experiences and EITHER occasionally supports these with evidence/reasons OR occasionally questions and answers relevantly.	Contributes a few ideas/responses/ opinions/experiences and these are only tenuously relevant.
ACCOUNT TAKEN OF OTHER CONTRIBUTIONS	Takes account of what others have to say in <u>several</u> of the following ways: by analysing/summarising/using/ expanding/supporting/challenging/ refuting their contributions.	On the whole, takes some account of what others have to say in <u>one</u> of the following ways: by summarising/using/expanding/ supporting/challenging their contributions.	Shows a few signs of taking account of what others have to say, in <u>one</u> of the following ways by repeating/using/supporting/ challenging their contributions.
AWARENESS OF SITUATION	Behaves in a way appropriate to the situation by: acknowledging the status of chair, leader, interviewer, etc; allowing/encouraging others to have their say; speaking readily, but not excessively; using language suited to the listener(s).	Behaves in a way appropriate to the situation by <u>two</u> of the following: acknowledging the status of chair, leader, interviewer, etc; allowing/encouraging others to have their say; speaking readily, but not excessively; using language suited to the listener(s).	Shows a few signs of attempting to behave in a way appropriate to the situation by <u>one</u> of the following: acknowledging the status of chair, leader, interviewer, etc; allowing/encouraging others to have their say; speaking readily, but not excessively; using language suited to the listener(s).
CONTROL OF EXPRESSION	Is consistently audible and clear <u>and</u> shows some skill in varying intonation to point up meaning and in adjusting pace to suit circumstances.	Is largely audible and clear <u>and</u> shows some signs of varying intonation to point up meaning or adjusting pace to suit circumstances.	Is in part audible and clear.

DIFFERENTIATING FACTORS	GRADE 1	GRADE 2	GRADE 3	GRADE 4	GRADE 5	GRADE 6
	Consistent, alert attention to purpose	Sound attention to purpose, but lacks some shrewdness, tenacity, subtlety.	Attention to purpose, is adequate	Attention to purpose, though impaired in some significant ways, just achieves adequacy required for General Level	Shows a few signs of attention to purpose	At least one audible intelligible attempt to contribute relevantly
	and	Performance is generally good, but is less fertile/less confident/less sensitive/less consistent than at grade 1	and	and	and	and
	combines some of the following features:		combines some of the following features:	combines some of the following features:	combines some of the following features:	shows some signs of willingness to co-operate in the discussion.
	high quality in contributions and taking account of what others say;		adequate substance and relevance of contribution;	substance and relevance of contribution;	a few contributions though weakened by irrelevance;	
	confidence of expression;		adequate account taken of other contributions;	account taken of other contributions;	some limited account taken of others;	
	tactful awareness of situation.		adequate awareness of situation;	awareness of situation;	some limited awareness of situation;	
	Overall, characterised by consistency of quality.		adequate control of expression.	control of expression.	reasonably audible and clear expression.	
				(One or more of these is impaired in some way but the combination just achieves overall adequacy.)		

TALKING (Individual Talk) GRC

	FOUNDATION	GENERAL	CREDIT
CONTENT	Expresses obvious and simple ideas. Displays little skill in linking ideas.	Expresses appropriate ideas. Links ideas with some skill.	Expresses ideas of quality, relevance and interest. Links ideas clearly to each other and to main purpose of task.
PURPOSE (as appropriate)	Presents simple facts, ideas or opinions with little attempt at sequencing. Gives a simple account of personal experience with a limited sense of involvement. In storytelling, sets the scene and outlines the narrative.	Conveys information in an orderly sequence. Orders and presents ideas and opinions with some attempt at reasoning. Gives a reasonably coherent account of a personal experience, expressing feelings and reactions with some sense of involvement. In storytelling, sets the scene, sustains narrative to its climax and conveys some sense of character.	Conveys information, highlighting what is most significant. Marshals ideas and evidence in support of argument. Gives succinct and coherent account of personal experience, with sensitive expression of feelings and reactions. In storytelling, achieves effect through creative use of structure, tone, timing, vocabulary and characterisation.
LANGUAGE	Uses a limited range of vocabulary and spoken language structures. Is restricted in register.	Uses vocabulary and spoken language structure which are largely accurate. Shows some awareness of appropriate register.	Uses varied and accurate vocabulary. Uses an appropriately wide range of spoken language structures. Uses a register appropriate to topic and audience.
EXPRESSION	Is, in part, audible and clear.	Is largely audible and clear. Displays some fluency. Shows some signs of ability to vary intonation to point up meaning or to adjust pace to suit the purpose.	Is consistently audible and clear. Is consistently fluent. Adjusts pace to suit purpose. Varies intonation to point up meaning.

	CREDIT		GENERAL		FOUNDATION	
AWARENESS OF AUDIENCE	Takes due account of the requirements and reactions of the audience. Makes appropriate use of eye contact, facial expression and gesture. Requires little or no prompting		Shows awareness of requirements and reactions of audience. Occasionally makes appropriate use of eye contact, facial expression and gesture. Requires some support through prompting and/or questioning.		Shows limited awareness of the requirements and reactions of audience. Requires substantial support through prompting and/or questioning.	
DURATION	Sustains talk at considerable length, as appropriate to purpose.		Sustains talk at some length, as appropriate to purpose.		Shows a limited ability to sustain talk, as appropriate to purpose.	
DIFFERENTIATING FACTORS	GRADE 1	GRADE 2	GRADE 3	GRADE 4	GRADE 5	GRADE 6
	Distinguished by a consistent and alert attention to purpose and combines some of the following features: high quality in content and language; confidence of expression; sensitive awareness of situation and audience. Overall, characterised by consistency of quality.	Sound attention to purpose, but lacks some sophistication, insight, fullness. Performance is generally good, but is less rich/less confident/less sensitive/less consistent than at grade 1.	Attention to purpose, is intermittent but adequate and combines some of the following features adequate content; adequate accuracy of language adequate expression; adequate awareness of audience.	Attention to purpose, though impaired in some significant way, just achieves the adequacy required for General Level. Despite weaknesses, the combination of qualities of content, language expression, awareness of audience just achieves overall adequacy.	Shows a few signs of attention to purpose and combines some of the following features: several items of content, though weakened by irrelevance and/or obscurity; intelligible language, weakened by inaccuracy; some limited awareness of audience; expression reasonably audible and clear.	Communicates a few intelligible ideas at least one of which is to the point

The GRC for Talking (pages 120 – 123) have one main subdivision. There are separate GRC descriptions for the two kinds of talk that are assessed at Standard Grade — Discussion and Individual Talk. Fortunately, these don't need to be explained at any great length since they are plainly enough stated. Don't think of the difference between them as being simply a matter of the number of people involved. Though that would be the natural way to think of it because of the use of the word 'individual' — "discussion equals many people talking: individual talk equals one person only" — it's only partly right. It will be more helpful to you if you can follow this line of thinking.

Talking is thought of as a 'continuum of interaction'. That may not be a familiar phrase, but it contains an idea that I'm fairly sure you already know. Think of the continuum as a scale of measurement where the gradations (the lines between one area and the next) are unmarked or vague: the sections merge into one another at the edges. At one end of this scale there is 'pure' listening: at the other there is 'pure' talking. You're probably already wondering where listening came from in this explanation of the standards for Talking. Just a reminder then that discussion has to involve listening. You can't really have anything that could be called discussion unless those taking part listen and then talk because of what they have listened to. So this 'continuum' or undivided line which measures 'interaction' really has to do with how much the people involved in the talking speak and how much they listen and speak to each other. Somewhere in the middle perhaps between the two extremes is a point at which both talking and listening are present, and in the correct mixture to form what we call discussion. The 'interaction' now doesn't need much more explanation. In this connection it means really the degree of talking that goes on among or between ('inter') the persons involved. So, of the 'continuum', one end of the scale — the 'pure listening' end, doesn't really have a part to play in the GRC for Talking; listening, by itself, isn't assessed in Standard Grade English any more: the other end — the 'pure talking' end of the continuum does have a very important part to play in the course and the assessment. The other part of the scale that is important stretches along the continuum from the pure talking end back towards the middle of the scale to a point where there is a mixture of talk and listening. So, the end of the scale is pure talking — at Standard Grade it's called Individual Talk and the middle is the mixture we are calling Discussion, and in Standard Grade this is certainly assessed. That is why there are GRC for Discussion.

To sum up (and there's also the diagram on page 125 to try to make it clearer), it's not really to do with how many people are involved in the talking: it's all to do with how much exchange (interaction) of talking goes on — that decides whether the talk is discussion or something else.

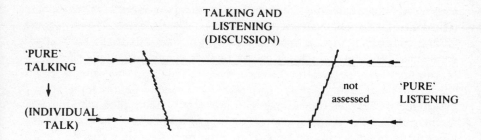

So, somewhere in the middle of continuum that you are probably now fed up hearing about (perhaps this section could have done with some re-drafting!), some Individual Talk will begin to look like Discussion: some Discussion will contain parts that tend to look remarkably like Individual Talk. What it means for you in practice is, for example, that you could be assessed for Individual Talk in the course of a discussion, perhaps, or you could be assessed for Discussion while you are exchanging opinions with perhaps only one other person — maybe a classmate, maybe your teacher. In most discussion, however, let's hope you will be taking turns talking and listening to several of your classmates and that for Individual Talk you'll be talking at some length to an audience of more than one person, usually your group or class.

In the GRC, this distinction is assumed to be a clear one, so that once it has been agreed what is going on, either Discussion or Individual Talk, the appropriate GRC are used for the assessing. There is a separate set of GRC for each, and they cannot both apply to any one activity. It's decided by the task which set fits and only those criteria are applied in assessing your talking work on any one occasion. The difference depends entirely on the amount of 'interactive' talk in the situation. The more there is, the more it is going to be Discussion; the less 'interactive' talk there is, the more it becomes Individual Talk. Interactive Talk is where those present in the talk situation actually talk to each other and listen to each other. Individual Talk is where one talks and the others listen but do not talk.

When we turn to look at the GRC for Talking (pages 120 – 123), you can see again that what you are actually expected to do is much the same at all three levels, but that the 'quality of performance', i.e. how well you do it, is different. The main thing to notice in the requirements at this stage is that Discussion makes special demands on you and how you deal with other people when you are discussing. I'm pointing this out to you carefully, because it's one part of Standard Grade English where your performance — and therefore your grade for Talking — can easily be affected by what other people do, or fail to do, and where their grade can be affected by what you do or fail to do. That is because Discussion is a co-operative task and activity. Look back to Chapter 6 for more about this. In the meantime, just think of any other co-operative activity — playing hockey or football, for instance, or being the trapeze artist in the circus who has to let go the trapeze and fly across to be caught by another member of the troupe. It depends on working with the others and on their working with you. Whether an individual performance is good or bad isn't the question any more if the team doesn't co-operate and the match or the circus act or the discussion ends in disaster.

The GRC I have printed here are simplified and set out like the other GRC showing all three levels and, as before, there is, below these, a list of the **differentiating factors** at each level, and these are used to decide on whether a performance at, say, General level should be assessed as Grade 3 or as Grade 4. Your teacher will be using a grid like this to assess what you have been able to do. The obvious problem in assessing talk is that it is all over so fast and leaves no permanent record of its having happened at all. Your teacher cannot sit down later with your talk and consider how to 'mark' it, in the way that he or she can do with your work in Reading or Writing, where what you have done is set down on paper. I know that we can make tapes of what was said, either audio-tapes or video-tapes, but that is not the whole of what goes on in talking. If you have another look at the GRC you will soon realise that. What the GRC are dealing with is what we could call 'talk behaviour': it isn't just about the sounds you make. Look at what the GRC have to say about other things: you can pick out words like 'awareness of situation', 'allowing', 'acknowledging', 'account taken'. These should make it clear to you that there is more to it than just talking in any old way. Discussion especially, is something that has to be learned, and you really do have to know what you are expected to do when you are discussing. This is what is dealt with in Chapter 6 on Talking.

Reading GRC

Now we come to the more complex set of GRC, for Reading. As you can see, they take up quite a few pages. You saw that there were **two** kinds of Talking: there are **three** kinds of Reading, and they need a separate set of GRC each.

READING — Extended Responses to Text

Critical Evaluations

In what follows the term "text(s)" should be taken to refer to poetry, drama and prose (both fiction and non-fiction) and also to films and radio and television programmes.

The quality of the text(s) chosen should allow the candidate to demonstrate the following skills.

	CREDIT	GENERAL	FOUNDATION
AS APPROPRIATE TO THE PURPOSE THE CANDIDATE	Displays a thorough familiarity with the text(s): this appears, e.g., in the analysis of its main ideas and purposes and through detailed reference to relevant areas of content Shows an ability to relate significant detail to the overall context of the work(s) studied.	Displays an acceptable familiarity with the text(s): this appears in a statement of its main ideas and purposes and through reference to some relevant areas of content. Shows some ability to relate detail to the overall context of the work(s) studied)	Displays some familiarity with the text(s): this appears in the statement of one or two of its main ideas and/or purposes and through reference to one or two relevant areas of content. Shows a little ability to relate detail to the overall context of the work(s) studied.
	Gives a perceptive and developed account of what s/he has enjoyed in/gained from the text(s): this clearly conveys the sense of a genuine personal response and is substantiated by reference to pertinent features of the text(s).	Makes a reasonably developed statement about aspects of the text(s) which have affected him/her: this conveys the sense of a genuine personal response and is accompanied by some reference to pertinent features of the text(s).	Makes a statement about at least one aspect of the text(s) that has affected him/her: this conveys traces of a genuine personal response.
	Demonstrates awareness of technique by analysis, using critical terminology where appropriate: this appears in full and perceptive explication of stylistic devices substantiated by detailed reference to the text(s) and, where appropriate, apt quotation.	Identifies individual features of technique and explains their effects, using basic critical terminology where appropriate: this involves the brief explication of obvious stylistic devices and is accompanied by some reference to the text(s) and/or quotation.	Identifies one or two features of technique which contribute to some obvious effect: this is accompanied by some reference to the text(s) and/or quotation.

	CREDIT		GENERAL		FOUNDATION	
AS APPROPRIATE TO THE PURPOSE THE CANDIDATE	Organises the response in such a way as to reflect, accurately, the purpose and nature of the assignment: this appears in an ability to select what is relevant in the text(s) and give due weight and prominence to what is important; the response is a substantial one but not normally exceeding 800 words.		Organises the response so as to take some account of the purpose and nature of the assignment: most of what is selected from the text(s) is relevant and adequate attention is given to what is important; the response is a reasonably extended one, probably between 300 and 600 words.		Displays some signs of awareness of the purpose and nature of the assignment: some of what is selected from the text(s) is relevant and a degree of attention is given to what is important; the response is at least 100 words in length.	
	GRADE 1	**GRADE 2**	**GRADE 3**	**GRADE 4**	**GRADE 5**	**GRADE 6**
DIFFERENTIATING FACTORS	Analysis of main ideas/purposes is thorough-going and precise	Analysis of main ideas/purposes is full but less penetrating than at grade 1.	Statement of main ideas/purposes is reasonably comprehensive and accurate.	Statement of main ideas/purposes is less complete/less correct than at grade 3.	Statement of main ideas/purposes displays a basic grasp.	Grasp of main ideas/purposes is tenuous.
	The account of personal reaction displays a high level of sensitivity and self-awareness	The account of personal reaction is discerning but less fully realised than at grade 1.	Statement of personal reaction displays a degree of insight.	Statement of personal reaction is more superficial and generalised than at grade 3.	Statement of personal reaction is brief but clear.	Statement of personal reaction lacks clarity but conveys a recognisable stance in relation to text(s).
	Use of critical terminology is confident and accurate.	Use of critical terminology is generally accurate but occasionally lacks the sureness of touch characteristic of grade 1.	Use of basic critical terminology is reasonably assured.	Awareness of critical terminology falters on occasion.	Awareness of technique is conveyed explicitly in simple non-technical language.	technique is detectable but tends to appear implicitly.
	There is an overall proportion and coherence in the structure of the response.	Everything is relevant to the purpose of the assignment but there is some disproportion of constituent parts.	There is clear reference throughout to the purpose of the assignment.	Sense of the purpose of the assignment is present but not explicitly acknowledged throughout.	There is at least one explicit reference to the purpose of the assignment.	Awareness of purpose appears briefly/implicitly.

READING — Extended Responses to Text

Imaginative Responses

In what follows the term "text(s)" should be taken to refer to poetry, drama and prose (both fiction and non-fiction).

The quality of the text(s) chosen should allow the candidate to demonstrate the following skills.

	CREDIT	GENERAL	FOUNDATION
AS APPROPRIATE TO THE PURPOSE THE CANDIDATE	Displays, as appropriate, a thorough familiarity with the text(s) through	Displays, as appropriate, an acceptable familiarity with the text(s) through	Displays, as appropriate, some familiarity with the text(s) through
	detailed allusion to relevant areas of content,	allusion to some relevant areas of content,	allusion to one or two relevant areas of content,
	sustained attention to the main ideas and purposes,	some attention to the main ideas and purposes,	and recognition of one or two of the main ideas and purposes.
	and sensitive evocation of mood and tone;	and occasional evocation of mood and tone;	
	awareness of technique appears through skilled deployment of appropriate stylistic devices.	some awareness of technique appears through the use of more obvious stylistic devices.	
	Organisation accurately reflects the purpose and nature of the assignment.	Organisation takes some account of the purpose and nature of the assignment.	There are some signs that account has been taken of the purpose and nature of the assignment.

130

DIFFERENTIATING FACTORS	GRADE 1	GRADE 2	GRADE 3	GRADE 4	GRADE 5	GRADE 6
	The candidate is confident and accomplished in the use of the chosen literary medium.	There are occasional lapses in control of the chosen literary medium.	The candidate displays some skill in using the chosen literary medium.	The candidate is less confident in using the chosen literary medium.	The candidate displays limited skill in using the chosen literary medium.	The candidate displays very little skill in using the chosen literary medium.
	The writing consistently demonstrates:	The writing demonstrates a high level of:	There is clear evidence of:	There is some evidence of:	There is little evidence of:	There are fleeting signs of:
	familiarity with the text(s);	familiarity with the text(s);	familiarity with the text(s);	familiarity with the text(s);	familiarity with the text(s);	familiarity with the text(s);
	awareness of technique;	awareness of technique;	awareness of technique;	awareness of technique;	awareness of technique;	awareness of technique;
	powers of organisation.	powers of organisation.	powers of organisation.	powers of organisation.	powers of organisaton.	powers of organisation.

131

READING — Extended Responses to Text

Close Reading

	CREDIT	GENERAL	FOUNDATION
TEXTS	Go beyond what is immediately accessible or related to personal interest and experience. Some feature unfamiliar, abstract ideas and complexity of structure and tone.	Accessible as a whole, mainly related to personal interest and experience, dealing with concrete human relationships or containing clearly presented ideas.	Brief and readily accessible, related to personal interest and experiences, dealing with concrete human relationships or containing clearly presented ideas.
THE CANDIDATE CAN	Make a clear concise statement of the main concerns of the text and show awareness of their relationships;	Make a clear statement of the main concerns of the text;	State the main concerns of the text;
	state accurately in his or her own words (where appropriate) and collate as required, items of information retrieved from the text;	state accurately in his or her own words (where appropriate) individual items retrieved from the text;	state accurately individual items of information from areas of the text which have been clearly defined;
	draw a precise inference from a key statement or statements, and substantiate this from evidence in the text;	draw a precise inference from a key statement in the text;	draw an acceptable simple inference from a key statement in the text;
	comment relevantly on some aspects of the author's point of view, and show some skill in justifying the comment from personal experience and knowledge and from evidence in the text;	comment relevantly on a clearly defined aspect of the author's point of view, and justify the comment from personal experience and knowledge and from evidence in the text;	comment simply and intelligibly on an aspect of the author's point of view that has been clearly defined and relate it to personal experience and/or knowledge;
	demonstrate some awareness of the author's technique by analysis, using critical terminology where appropriate.	identify individual features of the author's technique and explain their effects.	identify a feature (or features) of the author's technique which contributes to some clearly defined effect.

	GRADE 1	GRADE 2	GRADE 3	GRADE 4	GRADE 5	GRADE 6
DIFFERENTIATING FACTORS	The candidate demonstrates a sureness and sensitivity of understanding and appreciation in responding to particular questions on the various aspects of purpose. The responses are more consistent, more perceptive and more substantial (as required) than at grade 2.	While displaying as appropriate the characteristics essential for Credit Level, the candidate's responses are less consistent, less clear in perception and less full in explanation than at grade 1. Overall the performance is more uneven than at grade 1.	The candidate demonstrates a clear understanding and a sound appreciation in responding to particular questions on the various aspects of purpose. The responses are more consistant, more relevant and more successful in retrieving, paraphrasing, explaining and justifying than at grade 4.	While displaying as appropriate the characteristics essential for General Level, the candidate's responses are less consistent, less apt in illustration and explanations are less successful in retrieving, paraphrasing, explaining and justifying than at grade 3. Overall the performance is more uneven than at grade 3.	Demonstrates understanding and some appreciation in responding to particular questions on the various aspects of of purpose. The responses are more consistent more comprehensible and more specific than at grade 6.	While displaying as appropriate the characteristics essential for Foundation Level, the candidate is less consistent, less clear and more ambiguous in communicating responses than at grade 5. Overall the performance is more uneven than at grade 5.

In each set of GRC for Reading there is a statement for Foundation, General and Credit, but there are sub-divisions which were not found in the Summary GRC. The sub-divisions cover a number of things not yet explained to you, although they have been referred to.

Two Kinds of Reading

The first sub-division you can see here is that there are two main kinds of Reading:

1. Extended Responses to Reading (pages 128 – 131).
2. Close Reading (pages 132 – 133).

These are quite simple, really. If you recall that Reading is assessed in two ways, by means of work in the Folio, and by means of the external exam in Reading, you will quickly see why there are GRC statements for the two kinds mentioned just above.

1. Extended Responses to Reading are simply the kind of work you do when you write at length about what books or stories or poems, etc., you have been reading in class or at home. These Extended Responses (long answers) are the kind of pieces of writing that go into your Folio.

2. Close Reading is very like what you might already know as Interpretation. You read a passage or an extract and then you answer the questions printed after it. Close Reading is what you will be doing in the external examination. You will, of course, be doing this kind of work in class, too. The difference is that the kind of work you produce as a result of close reading will **not** go into your Folio. You'll be tested in this kind in the Board's written examination.

I hope you begin to see why half your grade for Reading comes from the Folio and half from the examination. They are each dealing with a different kind of reading. One of these (Extended Responses) is suitable for being done in class but marked at the Board: the other kind (Close Reading) could not be done like that but can be done in a national examination. This arrangement is designed to allow you to do the best kind of writing about your reading in the course, and at the same time make sure that the work of pupils all over the country is marked to the same consistent standard because they all answer questions about the same passage or passages. It's easy to understand if you think about it.

The Extended GRC set out the descriptions at all grades for each of these two kinds of Reading.

Difference between Levels

The second sub-division you can pick out is between LEVELS. In each of the sets of GRC you can see that there are sections for Credit, General and Foundation.

Difference between Grades

The third sub-division you can see is between grades at each level. Concentrating for the moment on the GRC at Foundation level (page 129) you will find "Differentiating Factors" at the end of the main description. In plain language, the main description covers the **Level**, i.e., Foundation: when you want to find the difference between a performance at grade 6 and one at grade 5 (both of these grades are in the Foundation Level), you look at the "differentiating factors" — the things that make the difference between them.

DIFFERENTIATING FACTORS . . .
Critical Evaluation — Foundation Level

" . . . make a statement about at least one aspect of the text(s) that has affected him or her . . ."

I said at the beginning that there are **two main** sub-divisions — Extended Responses and Close Reading. But there are **three** sets of GRC. That's because Extended Responses are divided further into two kinds.

So, the last sub-division appears only **within** the Extended Responses to Reading GRC. There, again taking the Foundation level GRC (pages 128 and 130) as an example, you will find that they give separate descriptions for the two kinds of writing you produce about the texts you have read in class:

1. Critical Evaluations.
2. Imaginative Responses.

More shorthand here, but not difficult to explain or understand.

1. *Critical Evaluations*

When you evaluate something you are simply placing a value on it, saying what significance it has, usually after careful study and thought. 'Critical' is clearly connected with 'criticize' — a much misunderstood word. It does **not** mean to complain about the faults of someone or something. It means, as used here, to judge. The word comes from a Greek word κριτεω meaning 'I judge'. So does 'criterion', a word we spent some time with earlier. So criticizing means considering both the merits and the faults, both sides of the case — 'judging'. A **critical evaluation** of a work of literature is a piece of writing which judges the merits and faults of the work and comes to a conclusion based on careful study and appraisal. You are quite familiar with this kind of writing. Your teacher will have asked you to produce such work before, though it's unlikely that he or she asked you to "write a critical evaluation of" whatever you have been reading. Although this is another piece of 'short-hand', it's as well that once you've understood what it means, you should go on using it, take it into your everyday vocabulary. Unbelievably, I really **mean** this. You will find it very useful when you are discussing your Folio work with your teacher and your classmates, believe it or not. It helps you to simplify the Folio requirements you read about earlier in this book (The Folio, Chapter 4).

2. *Imaginative Responses*

You've done this, too. It can take many forms, most of them familiar to you, I'm sure. Once you have read a work of literature — what the GRC call a 'text', your teacher may ask you as part of the work of a unit on, say, William Golding's novel, *The Lord of the Flies* to write a diary supposedly written by Piggy, one of the main characters in the novel. To do so, you require two things: knowledge of the text and creative imagination. You are responding imaginatively to the text.

You should be warned at this stage that there are very clear rules about what imaginative response you may include in your Folio and under what conditions. Ignoring the rules or the advice about this could have very bad consequences, i.e., not having your work graded because it does not meet the 'specification'. If you think you might want to include an imaginative response in the Reading part of your Folio, check very carefully the requirements given in the Folio chapter.

Close Reading

Look now at the GRC for Close Reading (pages 132 – 133).

There are no sub-divisions or other complications about these GRC. They describe the kind of overall performance in your written answers to questions on something you have read closely, i.e. a passage or extract provided with the questions. You will not have chosen the text: your teacher or the examiners will have chosen it for you.

The Close Reading GRC are mostly used for designing and setting Question Papers and this makes sure that you have the chance given to you to meet the purposes behind the questions. The GRC, however, are also **targets**, and you should use them to help you understand the kind of things you should be aiming at in your answers to questions in close reading. Notice words like "clear", "concise", "relevantly", "justifying", "accurately" and "evidence in the text".

There is a great deal more about close reading in the examination section earlier on in the book. Much of it has to do with the kind of examination papers you will sit, but don't forget that you will also be doing various kinds of close reading in the class and so what is said there about the exam applies to that coursework as well.

The GRC are not meant to be read as a continuous story: let's face it, that would not be the most fascinating read of all time. They are intended for *reference*, obviously. You look up the part you want to know about at the time you want to know about it. Normally they would have been printed as an Appendix at the end of a book like this: I have deliberately chosen to print them at this point so that you have them beside the information and explanation you have just been reading. Later, you can look up the particular section you need to know about at any time.

If you have to use a dictionary for some of this jargon, then do so. It's hard work, but the more you study the GRC against your own work, the more you will understand about how Standard Grade works — and that alone is going to help you to do better in the end.

CHAPTER 9

THE CERTIFICATE

This one really **is** brief: I promise. Its only purpose is to let you see what the certificate looks like. It isn't possible to show you a real one in all its glory. It is more than twice this size, and is printed in colour, with the paper sealed in a laminated plastic covering — not just to make it look nice, but also to make it impossible to alter it once it has been issued. You'd be surprised ... .

So the certificate on the next page is a specimen for a fictitious candidate from a fictitious school. William Bruce Wallace must be in S5 at Stirlingbridge Academy, because the certificate includes awards on the Higher Grade. The interesting points are the four subjects at Standard Grade. Under the *Profile of Performance* you can see what he got for each of the **elements** and how these have been aggregated (added together) and the Award for the subject obtained. Listening is included in English, but your exam and certificate won't show it.

It doesn't perhaps look like very much for all that work, but it simply represents proof to others of what you have achieved. I hope that you will have gained a great deal of satisfaction from your Standard Grade course, along with some enjoyment along the way, and that you gain a certificate like this one. Whatever kind of a certificate you are awarded, you will have had a valuable and unforgettable experience.

Scottish Certificate of Education

SPECIMEN   *The Scottish Examination Board hereby certifies that* WILLIAM BRUCE WALLACE

SPECIMEN   *presented for the Scottish Certificate of Education* in 1987 by STIRLINGBRIDGE ACADEMY

obtained at the Examination in that year the following award(s):

Subject	Grade	Award	Profile of Performance (Standard Grade Only)	
ART AND DESIGN	Ordinary	4		
ENGLISH	Standard	1 *	Reading	1
			Writing	2
			Listening	1
			Talking	1
MATHEMATICS	Standard	2	Interpreting & Communicating Information	2
			Selecting a Strategy	2
			Processing Data	1
			Problem solving	3
			Practical Investigations	3
SCIENCE	Standard	‡	Knowledge and Understanding	5
			Handling Information	4
			Problem Solving	4
SECRETARIAL STUDIES	Ordinary	3		
SHORTHAND 60 WPM	—	—		
SOCIAL AND VOCATIONAL SKILLS	Standard	3	Social & Communication Skills	3
			Practical Skills	4
			Problem Solving & Decision Making Skills	2
GERMAN	Higher	C		
ITALIAN	Higher	B		
MUSIC PARTS I, II AND IV	Higher	A		
MUSIC (PRACTICAL HARMONY)	—	—		

* *Special provision has been made for the candidate to an extent requiring endorsement of the certificate. Details of the provisions made are available from the Board on request.*

‡ *The candidate has been graded only in the element(s) shown in the Profile of Performance because one or more of the element grades required for an overall award is missing. This may be due to circumstances outwith the candidate's control.*

4/1234567–12345   SPECIMEN SPECIMEN SPECIMEN SPECIMEN SPECIMEN SPECIMEN   *Director*

140

The piece of writing that follows is genuine, though anonymous. It was not written by me, but by a real pupil. My colleague, Ken Cunningham, in his book on *Reading for Standard Grade English*, invented a pupil called Malcolm. Let's call the writer of this piece Donalbain. Some of you will recognize that as a pretty awful joke. What Donalbain has written is what a manufacturer would call a 'product endorsement' or an 'unsolicited testimonial', and shows what he thinks about the Standard Grade course he has been doing.

STANDARD GRADE ENGLISH

I am definitely for Standard Grade. The old O' Grade courses need to be changed and I think that S.G. reaches all requirements. Old courses relied too much on recall, I didn't mind that, but it wasn't really fair. If you have a good memory then you're sailing. S.G. involves much more problem solving, in every-day life situations. This gives those with poor memories a better chance of passing exams. It also requires more skill.

At first I wasn't very keen on S.G. probably because I have a pretty good memory but now that I have actually done some of the work in English and Maths I just love it! I find the new courses much more interesting and lively especially in English. You don't seem to notice it so much in maths.

One of the main aspects of S.G. English that I enjoy is group work. Some of the slower members may hold the group back, but not that much and anyway most people enjoy helping those slower than themselves. I'm not sure I like the teachers picking the groups, but then I would hate it if we picked our own groups. What I think is that we should each have at least one good friend in the same group. Group work, I approve of, because it brings out leadership qualities in people. It teaches them to talk freely expressing their opinions, to discuss, to argue and to listen.

S.G. English also involves more practical work like talking, listening and watching relevant films. I enjoy doing this as it livens up the lesson, gets you interested, improves your skills and teaches you.

I also approve of work being set by the teachers, even if they don't like the extra work. The teacher can choose work which will interest the pupils and him/herself and bring out the best in pupils. I think it also gives the teacher more satisfaction at the end of the day to know that they didn't rely on text books, but did something which required much more skill. That is to 'write their own text book'.

In S.G. English you will get a certificate however poorly you do. Some people may look on a certificate saying that you are a 'failure' as something awful, but I think it gives a person a feeling of security and pleasure at actually having followed a course and having got something for it.

I like the idea of slim folios, where only your 'crème de la crème' goes. Everyone should be proud to a certain extent of their folios. It gives a better chance to the pupil to have two years to produce a certain amount of work, than to get a high grade in a paper which they have never seen before and in a short time will be taken away.

So far I have enjoyed Standard Grade English and cannot think of any faults, (I probably will after I hand this in!) or anything else to say, so I will wind-up by saying once again. It's a big improvement and I love it!

CHAPTER 10

HIGHER ENGLISH

If you gain a Grade 1, 2 or 3 at Standard Grade English and move into S5, as you are very likely to do (more and more pupils do so every year) you will have the chance to take a course leading to Higher English.

If you have enjoyed the way of working at Standard Grade, you will be well prepared for the Higher Grade course and its examinations. The Higher course has been revised since 1988 to make it fit better with Standard Grade, though hardly any pupils have taken it yet (the first 4000 or so in 1989). Instead of taking three exams in Composition, Interpretation and Language, and Literature, you will sit only two, one called Reading, and the other Writing.

The third part of the exam will allow you to produce work in your own time during the course in school and at home, in a Folio of Personal Studies. This contains a Review of Personal Reading (which means just that: you choose) and either Imaginative or Discursive Writing. These, as you can see, are terms you already know from Standard Grade. The clear intention of Higher is to refine and extend what you have done and learned at Standard Grade.

The exam papers contain close reading and critical evaluation, practical criticism, transactional writing (conveying information) and opportunities for the close study of literature.

I hope that this book will go a little way to helping you to survive the Standard Grade course, emerge the better for it, ready to tackle Higher.

Printed by Bell and Bain Ltd., Glasgow